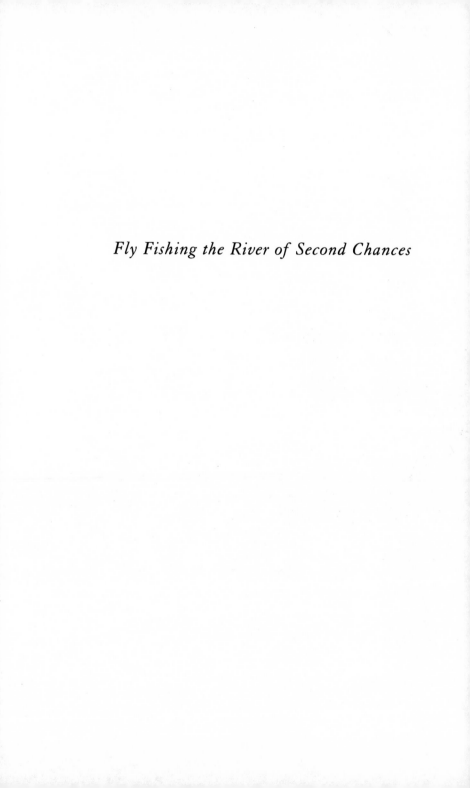

Fly Fishing the River of Second Chances

Sept 03

For my new friend Tony —
you are an inspiration. I
appreciate your sincerity and
devotion to your work. Don't
keep your thoughts and
writings a secret — because your
audience and I want to
know what they are.

Jennifer

JENNIFER OLSSON

Fly Fishing the River

of

Second Chances

**LIFE, LOVE, AND A
RIVER IN SWEDEN**

ST. MARTIN'S PRESS 〰 NEW YORK

www.stmartins.com

Book design by Kate Nichols

Illustration on page ix by Mikael Larsson

ISBN 0-312-31315-2

First Edition: October 2003

10   9   8   7   6   5   4   3   2   1

FOR EVA OLSSON

My Friend

Contents

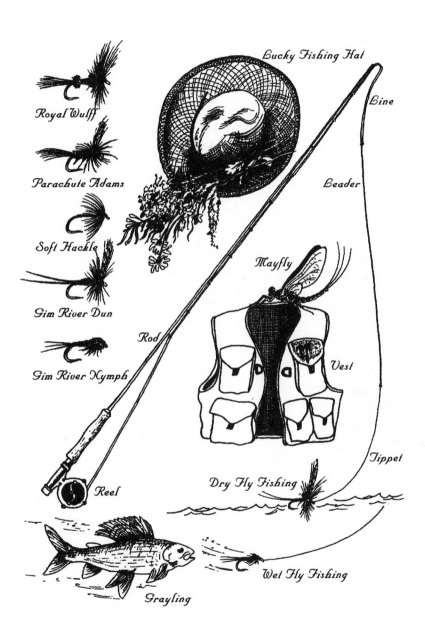

Royal Wulff

Parachute Adams

Soft Hackle

Gim River Dun

Gim River Nymph

Lucky Fishing Hat

Line

Leader

Mayfly

Rod

Vest

Tippet

Reel

Dry Fly Fishing

Wet Fly Fishing

Grayling

Fly Fishing the River of Second Chances

How It All Began

THE 2 A.M. PHONE CALL rang me right out of a dreamless sleep. Each ring seemed to toll my greatest fears: A brother, a sister, a father, or a friend was in trouble—or worse. I tossed back the covers, left my sleeping husband, and hurried down the hall to my office, where the phone sat next to the computer on a desk cluttered with papers, books, and photographs. I reached for the receiver just as the answering machine clicked into action, then hesitated. I wasn't really ready for a tear-choked voice to make an announcement. Thirty more seconds would help steel me for what was to come. I prepared to respond with all the calm I could muster. "Dad's in the hospital"—*I'll be on the next plane*; "Tim's been in a car wreck"—*I'll be on the next plane*; "Carrie's been kidnapped"—*I'll be on the next plane*; "Tom's had an aneurysm"—*I'll be on the next plane. I'm coming, I'll be there, I'll catch the next plane.*

Maybe it wasn't a crisis. Maybe it was just a drunk who had dialed the wrong number. Hugging myself in the dark and watching the blinking green light of the machine, I waited. One click later, a soothing voice with a British accent floated into the room.

"Hello, this is Lars Olsson calling from Sweden. I got your letter and was hoping to talk with you about . . ."

I couldn't believe it. I had sent this Swedish man a letter two weeks earlier, telling him that I couldn't accept his invitation to come fish his river in northern Sweden. I'd thanked him, but my no had been firm. And here he was again. His English was much better than I had thought it would be. However, it was obvious he had not grasped the time difference between Bozeman, Montana, and his little town, whose name I couldn't just then recall.

". . . teaching a fly-fishing course for women on my river here near the village of Gimdalen."

I had lived and worked as a fly-fishing guide for over seven years, along with my husband, who was also a fishing guide; we were parents of a young boy. Being one of the few professional women in the sport, I would often get calls to guide women or to come teach at fishing schools. But Lars Olsson's request to teach an all-women's course in Sweden had come as a surprise, for the fly-fishing world outside the boundaries of Montana was completely unknown to me. According to my smug way of thinking, Montana was *the* top fly-fishing destination in the world. Where was Sweden, exactly, and what kind of fish—besides, say, herring—did they have there anyway?

I had gotten Olsson's letter of invitation two months earlier. I remember pulling the tan-colored envelope with colorful stamps—honoring the Swedish Queen Sylvia on them—out of the post office box, thinking, *I don't know anyone in Sweden.* I was used to receiving letters from potential clients requesting information about guide trips or brochures; this was my first international letter. Intrigued, I tore open the envelope when I got back in the car and read:

Dear Jennifer,

I have got your name and business brochure from C. L. of England. I met him at his fly shop when I went over from Sweden to give a talk about grayling fishing at the Grayling Society's annual symposium and dinner. He said you were an experienced fly-fishing guide and casting instructor.

I have an idea about the interest for fly fishing and teaching fly fishing that we both share. But let me tell you first about myself!

My home village is Gimdalen with 110 inhabitants, in the forest country, in the middle of Sweden, close to the river Gim where I have been teaching fly fishing since the last ten years, even at school when I was a teacher.

The fishing in my area has taken a great step toward a fishing of high quality by restoring the river Gim after damage from the timber logging. They have prohibited the use of worms and the most important step, made me a riverkeeper by letting me lease one of their streams in the river Gim. There I now control the fishing completely and have started to make a fly-only-water on the section of the Gim called Idsjöströmmen with a limited number of fly fishers every day. Idsjöströmmen is 1,300 yards long and 30–50 yards broad and is home to brown trout and the "lady of the stream"—grayling.

I noticed here in Gimdalen last year that more and more women accompanied their boyfriends or husbands instead of sitting at home reading a book or knitting. So I think it is a good idea to start doing something special for the women interested in fishing.

Would you be interested to come to Sweden, to Gimdalen to fish my river, Idsjöströmmen, and to Tjuonajokk fishing camp and be a part of this fly fishing for women project? For instance 3–4 days in Gimdalen working/teaching together with me and 4–5 days at Tjuonajokk?

It is probably that the next season will be best, because we need time for marketing and advertising, but I feel that we lose one year. It would be interesting to see if we can be useful to each other, for you to feel the atmosphere, to see what the rivers look like and if you like it at all! And, most important, what would the costs for you be?

I look forward to hearing from you, your questions and ideas.

Best regards,
Lars Olsson
Riverkeeper/Idsjöströmmen

"What is he, nuts?" I had said out loud, tossing the letter onto the passenger seat, where it landed on top of a pile of junk mail that would go in the trash as soon as I got home. I couldn't just take off for Sweden in the middle of the fishing season. Didn't he understand how far away I lived? And what's with this fish called grayling—this "lady of the stream"? I had actually seen pictures of grayling in books. They looked like a whitefish with a big dorsal fin; not pretty, in my opinion. Besides, after appearing in several magazine articles about women fly fishers I had received some strange invitations from lonely men eager to show me around their home waters. A few had even sent photos of themselves holding trophy-sized fish. I had learned to be careful. I fully intended to ignore his request, but three months later when his letter resurfaced among papers on my cluttered desk, I decided to send a reply.

Dear Lars,

Thank you for your letter. Please forgive my very late response to your request. After giving your proposal careful thought I have to say I'm sorry I won't be able to come to Sweden this year. As a fishing guide here in Montana I am fully booked for the summer and must plan my summers a year in advance.

I think what you are doing sounds interesting. I hope all goes well with you this summer.

Sincerely,
Jennifer

That, as they say, should have been that. However, as soon as I had dropped the letter into the mail slot at the post office I had sighed with regret. Once upon a time I would gladly have jumped on a plane to just about anywhere. *Maybe even Sweden,* I thought, as I listened to Lars Olsson leaving his message on our machine.

———

WHEN I WAS A YOUNG GIRL, living with my parents and my older brother, Tom, in Long Beach, California, there were no difficulties getting me into the car for a camping or fishing trip. Escaping our suburban neighborhood, where crossing the street required permission from our mother, traveling to Montana, Wyoming, and the High Sierras was freedom itself. By the time I was eleven, I was familiar with fly fishing, horsepack trips, river rafting, and sleeping under the stars.

Just before I turned twelve, my parents took my brother and me to an outdoor trade show being held at the Long Beach Convention Center. There I saw a slide presentation put on by a man named Bo, who ran a wilderness camp near Butte, Montana. The slides showed conical-shaped tents staked to a land that rolled out under an overarching blue sky. White-capped peaks rose in the background; gray smoke curled up from campfires. Bo told us that campers would learn to live in the woods. The camp would offer opportunities to ride horses, fish, shoot, tour Yellowstone Park, and raft the Salmon River in Idaho.

I was transported. I saw myself galloping bareback on an Appaloosa across the Montana landscape, the reins in one hand, a .22 rifle blazing away at gophers in the other, the wind whipping through my long auburn hair.

When the lights came on, my parents signed Tom up for Bo's camp on the spot.

"This isn't for you, Jennie. You're too young," they told me.

The corners of my mouth slid south and stayed there for the rest of the day, into the night, and through the following week.

"Stubborn" is what my family called me, and stubborn I was. I was determined to step into the scene of those tents and horses and rivers, even if I had to walk to Montana to do it. I begged my parents, I stalked them, and I didn't stop until the deposit for the camp had been torn from the checkbook. They knew there would be no peace until they sent their pouting teenage daughter to the wilds of Montana.

And so I went to Bo's camp. After two weeks' training in survival techniques—learning how to keep warm and dry, start a fire, identify edible plants, and read a map and a compass—campers were permitted to sign up for a solo expedition. This meant choosing a destination in a wilderness area, hiking to it alone, staying overnight, and hiking out the next day. We were all eager to pass our solo expedition and carry home the certificate proving we had done it, but I was particularly eager. I was the youngest in camp, one of three girls out of twenty-one kids, and I did not want to fail.

Off I went, armed only with matches, a plastic tarp for shelter, a hacksaw, a mess kit, a canteen of water, a knife, a packet of salt, and a box of Kraft's Macaroni & Cheese, which was to be used only in case of emergency. My jacket and the clothes I hiked in offered the only protection from the elements. Sleeping bags were not permitted. We could, however, take along a book. Anybody who didn't eat the emergency rations was considered tougher than the rest.

I hiked into the Pintlar Wilderness Area and chose my campsite next to a creek. I had been taught how to peel off an inner slice of tree bark for sustenance; it tasted like turpentine jerky. I tried nibbling on the roots of dogwood flowers. After two hours of hiking, my hunger was very real—exceeding the need to be considered tough—so I made plans to cook up the macaroni and cheese for dinner.

This required fire. After draping my tarp between two large boulders, and securing it with rocks, I sawed pine boughs to lay on the ground on which I would sleep. Next I sawed wood for a fire. This kept my mind off the bears. I had been told that animals were afraid of fire and would stay away. My plan was to have enough wood to keep a fire lit all night long. By late afternoon, I had seven large logs and a big pile of cut branches and dry twigs.

I boiled the water and cooked the macaroni and cheese, which I ate to the very last bite, then licked the pot. The fire was my companion. The flames entertained me, the smell of burning pine soothed. The boulders became warm from the fire, and after reading a few chapters of the book I had stashed in my backpack—I fell asleep, my jacket draped over my shoulders.

In the morning I lingered at my camping place. Except for being hungry, I was beginning to get comfortable with this wilderness. I had learned I could get by on very little. Nature was nothing to be afraid of; it was a comfort, and it had strengthened my sense of self. I knew I could survive in the natural world. Later there would be times when I would forget about that snug place between the boulders, the fire burning all night, and my fears would grow bigger than bears.

Part of the reason my parents had finally given in and let me go to Bo's camp was to give my mother some rest. She had breast cancer. Neither Tom nor I knew this. Our parents, trying to spare us a dose of harsh reality, had put off telling us. They thought she would get better and didn't want to frighten us. Tom and I went about the business of marching into adolescence unaware that we were hiking along a precipice.

Soon after I had returned from Bo's wilderness camp, things started to change. My mother stopped driving her car. Months earlier, my father had bought her a brand-new Lincoln Continental with a light-green body and a dark-green vinyl roof. It had a dark leather interior, air conditioning, and electric windows, which my brother and I raised and lowered until she told us to *stop it or we'd break something.* I found it strange that anything about this massive car, piloted by a woman of such breathtaking beauty and strict discipline, could possibly break. But my mother got weaker and weaker, and when she had become too weak to trust her reflexes, she parked the Lincoln in the garage. My father drove it to work once a week to keep the battery charged.

What I remember being told about my mother's illness was that she had a bad back. When people asked me how my mother was, I'd say that her back was bothering her. When I told this to the mother of a friend, she tilted her head.

"Her back?"

"Yes, she has a sore back," I replied.

The woman's face took on a strange look, something between pain and confusion. She remained silent about what she knew, the kind of thing that women in neighborhoods know, and joined the protective circle shielding my brother and me from our mother's *cancer.*

My mother took to staying in bed all day; and when she got up, she hobbled around on crutches in her bathrobe. I would come home from school—I was in the sixth grade—

and sit next to her. Sometimes I combed her raven-black, shoulder-length hair. I'd carefully part it down the middle with the tip of the comb (not too hard or I'd hurt her scalp), then braid and secure two plaits with plastic toggled hair bands. Her dark hair, tanned skin, and high cheekbones reminded me of a Native American woman; I called this her Sacajawea hairdo.

She taught me how to use the electric shaver and I loved to buzz it up her long beautiful, unblemished legs. When she wanted a massage she asked me to warm the cream with my hands before rubbing it onto her back, arms, legs, and hands. Afterward I would sit with my mother, tell her about my day at school or my friends. I'd bring her apple juice and toast, then skip off to do my homework.

Mary, our housekeeper, came to the house in the early morning, and prepared three meals a day. She usually left before my father, an attorney, came home from work. If he was late, my brother and I put a portion of the dinner Mary had prepared for our mother on a tray and took it to her. On a good day, she might manage to make it to the dinner table and eat with us. On a bad day, after Mary had left, she could be heard crying. At first it sounded as if she had a cold and was sniffling. Then the sounds of heartfelt sobbing came, the ragged inhalations and sorrowful exhalations, and I would hesitate outside her door, afraid to go in and yet afraid to leave her in there by herself.

Toward the end I didn't know was coming came an afternoon when the pain my mother had tried not to complain about erupted. She cried uninhibitedly, like a woman giving birth. Being older and braver, my brother went in first. Our mother was on her side in the middle of the bed.

"Why doesn't he come home? Where is he?" she said pleadingly, and then groaned in agony.

We called our father's office but he wasn't there.

"He left the office. He's on the way," I remember telling her, without really knowing. I got on the bed next to her and pulled back the hair that was stuck to her face by her tears. She wanted heat to help the spasms in her back, her legs, her neck. Tom began soaking washcloths in hot water. Together we carried warm, wrung-out washcloths from the bathroom sink and pressed them gently against her skin. Our father finally arrived, and he quickly administered some kind of analgesic. That night our mother never stopped weeping.

In the morning, my tall father lifted my frail mother from her bed and carried her effortlessly outside. One of my mother's arms hung loosely around my father's neck, the other weakly gripped the front of his shirt. He had zipped up her bathrobe and put slippers on her feet. Her braids were loose, but the bands still held. For the first time since the day before, she was not crying—just looking. She looked back at the house she and my father had built as a young couple and had brought their babies home from the hospital to. I don't know if she saw me or not, but I stood at the window where she could have seen me, afraid to wave good-bye.

My father walked quickly but carefully to the garage so that he could place her in the backseat of the Lincoln and rush her to the hospital. I saw my father twist the garage door handle, then shoulder the door open before pressing his back against it to bring my mother through without bumping or scraping her against the door frame. In one swift movement my father spun her into the darkness. The door slammed shut behind them. And she was gone.

That summer my mother died, some childhood friends of my father's invited us to join them and their families for a two-week fly-fishing vacation near Ennis, Montana. In late June a plane carrying two thin, tired, self-conscious teenagers and their weary father landed in West Yellowstone. As we stepped down from the aircraft, the sharp chill of fresh, smogless air snapped us to attention. Being Californians, my brother and I had packed our jackets and arrived in jeans and thin cotton T-shirts. I dashed into the gas-station–sized terminal to get warm.

A station wagon carried us along Highway 20 into the upper reaches of Idaho, then into Montana, after we had crossed Reynolds Pass Bridge over the sparkling waters of the Madison River. My father pulled over and got out to have a look. My first impression of the river was one that might be expected from any underdressed thirteen-year-old girl.

"Fine. It's cold. I'm going back to the car."

But even in my edgy teenage state I felt something tugging at me. The sights and smells and the raw feeling of the outdoors on my skin felt familiar; only a year before, a hundred or so miles north of where we were parked, I had tromped the woods and slept alone in them. I had been fearless then in a landscape once so inviting.

Our next stop was just south of Ennis, near an area called the Channels, where a ranch family rented several houses on their property to summer guests. Between the Wallace family—my father's childhood friends—and their thirteen assorted children, ranging in ages from five to teenage, plus other adult guests of the Wallaces, we filled the place to capacity. Of the three buildings occupied by our group, the cedar-sided bunkhouse to the north was reserved for the boys—all nine of them. In the middle, a remodeled log barn was designated the main lodge for the adults; the ranchette to the south was for the four girls.

All the hunger, demands, and energy that such a wide spectrum of kids created was handily organized and dealt with by the mothers. It was scary to have a committee of women telling me what I could do and when I could eat, their voices firm and decisive. The other kids, being brothers, sisters, and cousins, were used to being corralled in this way, and they played hard within the perimeters of their marked off territory. Peas were flipped across the table, middle fingers darted up, and an art was made of put-downs.

At first I tried not to show my wide-eyed worry that we would get in trouble, but I soon learned that the mothers were on vacation when it came to the content of our conversation— and as long as we kept quiet enough we could snort, recite naughty limericks, and kick each other under the table to our hearts' content.

The adults ate together, no doubt to avoid the theater we would have provided for them, and as soon as the last kid took the last slug of milk, and was safely out the door, their lives as adult beings came into focus. Glasses of wine were poured, the best cuts of beef were grilled, and they started up their own brand of hilarity.

Sometimes I hung around the front porch with a few of the other stragglers listening to the wavelike rise and fall of our parents' voices as storytelling and jokes were shared. I got a chill when I heard the high and free sound of one of the women responding to something one of the men had said. I turned quickly and pressed close to the panoramic window that opened onto the porch to see what was going on. I thought she might be crying, but when I saw that everyone around her was smiling, I realized that she was laughing.

When the adults had finished their dinner, and we could catch the scent of cigar smoke wafting over the lawn, we knew we might have a better chance of sneaking into the main lodge, where access to the secret world of our parents would be possible. What made it easier was that the Scotch was open, and a card game might be getting under way. The mothers would have finished the dishes, parked a bottle of wine on the coffee table in front of the sofa, and be heavily engaged in the sharing of personal opinions on everything from current events to whether or not sex was better after a hysterectomy.

We learned to quietly crack open the front door and make a beeline for our fathers. Near our fathers we were closer to their powers, which as far as we were concerned, turned the world on its axis. They were handsome and tall and tough. Our fathers were educated western men who knew how to drink and joke, hike and fish, attract beautiful women for wives, and wear a jacket and tie when the occasion required. Our fathers had grown up together in the same neighborhood, played together as children, took trips with each other's families during the summers—just as they were doing with us. We sat behind their chairs, or if we were small we crept into their laps, and eavesdropped on their storytelling as they played cards while puffing away on cigars. They were all Stanford fraternity brothers and told fond, exaggerated stories of the trouble they had gotten into on drunken weekends, playing pranks on professors, and of their almost deadly experiments with explosives in abandoned barns. They were brutally witty—*goddamns* and *hells* punctuated their conversation, and we loved their quipped responses to each. It was deliciously dangerous being in their company, and they let us hang around them like grapes while they amused each other and us.

Every morning the fathers were up early, regardless of the late hour they went to bed, planning the day's fishing.

"How about going up to Three-Dollar Bridge? Hell, on a day like today there's got to be some good fishing up there on caddis. Then tomorrow we could take a day trip to the Gravelly Range and fish the Ruby."

Coffee cups in hand they'd head out to the front porch and begin suiting up in the latest wader technology available—Hodgemen bootfoot waders with felted soles. Fenwick or Winston fly rods would be chosen, Pflueger or Hardy reels to go with them. After that they would search through the pockets of fishing vests for Maxima tippet material, so they could begin attending to knotted, shortened, or broken leaders.

The nearsighted propped their glasses on their foreheads, then turned and twisted the transparent tippet into fresh clean knots. Sometimes when tested by a strong steady pull, the new knots popped and a low grumble or a whispered swearing followed.

All the boys, except the five-year-old, had an open invitation to fish with the fathers. They were present on the porch as well, rigging their fly rods, accusing each other of pilfering vest pockets during the night for leader and flies, racing to see who would get to the car first.

Every morning I watched the men and the boys at their ritualistic preparations. My dad and my brother swept up in the commotion and excitement didn't notice my serious silent figure standing next to them. I knew a little bit about fishing with a fly rod. I had been offered the chance on various family camping trips into the Trinity Alps and the Sierra Mountains in California. I'd felt the freedom of wading barefoot along the edges of tumbling mountain creeks, the mysterious, almost electrical connection to a trout on the end of my line, and I liked it.

Just as I was getting up the courage to ask my father to include me in on some of the fun, a mother would appear and gently steer me by the shoulder through the front door of the lodge and insist I eat breakfast or go hungry until lunch. My excursion that day would be to continue riding the fat and sassy quarter horses the generous ranch owners had given the girls access to.

Jill and I were the oldest of the four girls and we both approached riding with fearless enthusiasm. No saddles or stirrups or helmets for us. A hackamore bit, and the strength to hold onto a tuft of mane kept us seated throughout our many walking, trotting, galloping adventures. In one nearby pasture a Hereford bull (complete with iron ring through the nose) stood guard over his cows. We decided it would be sporting to challenge him to a game of chicken. To make it more interesting we dismounted our horses and slowly walked toward him. With thumbs in our ears we wagged our fingers, stuck out our tongues, made threatening sounds, then shook our butts at him. The bull responded by snorting, pawing, and putting on a frightful display of aggression until we got too close and he ran back toward his cows, all fifteen of them staring blankly in our direction.

When we weren't harassing the cattle, we were swimming our horses in the Madison River, or else combing and brushing and braiding our steeds like enormous living dolls. It was all great fun, but at unexpected moments I felt confused and afraid and lost. I'd suddenly tire of riding and want to go back to the main house and be around the mothers who were comfortably situated in various states of recline on the front porch, where they pulled colorful threads through their needlework canvases, read current novels, or chatted quietly in the shade. I went there to be within earshot of their voices, and to wait for my father to return.

Near six or seven in the evening, the sunburned men and their sons would roar back into sight, dust flying behind the train of station wagons as they pulled up to the lodge. Daughters and wives appeared on cue to welcome the conquering fishermen home. Car doors sprang open and out tumbled reports on the number and size of fish caught almost before arms and legs had been untangled and put into synchronized movement with their rightful owners. Congratulations were poured over the boys who had caught fish and they grew quietly satiated with the praise of their adoring mothers.

The boys stampeded to the dinner table and the evening's raucous fun began again. Each fish caught needed a Homeric tale to describe the saga behind its foiling and the crowded dinner table rose in volume as boys battled to be heard. Jill and I sat with the other girls and the five-year-old. No one was interested in our day: that we had walked up to a bull and called its bluff.

Every time I watched my dad and brother drive away with the rest of the group, I felt my world disappearing. I was supposed to eat when told to eat, play when told to play, stay out of the way, and be happy. The idea, I'm sure, was to assimilate me into normal everyday life as quickly as possible. But losing my mother only weeks before, then losing the companionship of my father and brother on a daily basis was about as much abandonment as I could tolerate.

One morning while I quietly studied the fishing preparations on the front porch, a familiar hand on my shoulder started to steer me through the lodge door toward the breakfast table.

"Don't bother your father right now."

I shrugged the hand off my shoulder with an exaggerated roll of my arm and marched over to my father who was seated on a bench trying to repair his leader.

"I want to go with you."

My father looked up at me, his bushy gray eyebrows arched skyward.

"You can come if you want. You'll have to hurry. You'll have to get some warmer clothes. The wind blows and you'll get cold wading wet."

I dashed to get more clothes. Soon I was in the car, wedged between boys that smelled of sweat and peanut-butter toast.

When we reached the Madison River, we were instructed to link arms for the crossing to desirable runs and pools on the other side. I silently suffered the sting of cold water as we waded. The river pushed our thin hips, slipped our feet over polished stones, and spit us out laughing and shivering on the other side. The boys ran off in one direction. I followed my father in another. He patiently tied a Royal Wulff fly onto the end of my leader. Next he reminded me how to cast, then showed me how to float the fly over the seam lines behind protruding rocks, through runs, upstream, across, and against the edge of an island of overgrown willows.

"Now you work this area, and if you finish, work it again. I'll be upstream. Call if you need some help."

With that, he ambled away, already absorbed in his search for a good run to cast to. A little chilled from the soaking wade I stood facing the river.

The northern and southern horizons appeared far and distant. To the east the landscape began in the high, rugged, snowy peaks of the Madison Range, tumbled down over foothills, then poured out into the golden and green Madison Valley. To the west the slope of the land rose again until it peaked in the Gravelly Range, dipped, then peaked again toward the north in the Tobacco Root Range. Spread out before me were miles and miles of uninhabited terrain, their possibilities endless. I felt thrilled and at the same time anxious stepping off the bank into the river. The breeze was scented by sagebrush and cottonwoods as I made my first cast over the water.

When the rainbow trout took, yanking the line from my clumsy hands, I was a little frightened. I reeled the wrong way then reversed. As soon as the trout seemed close, I tossed the rod down on the ground and proceeded to hand-over-hand the line until I caught sight of an agitated shadow below the water's surface. My father had witnessed my catch and dashed to my side, net in hand. With the same swift motion a bear uses to swat a salmon, my father scooped up my trout.

Not only did I feel I had done something of consequence and received my father's attention, I had been reminded that even when I couldn't see life it was there, beneath the currents, tucked under the cut banks, in the shadows, waiting to be discovered.

Beginning Again

MY LIFE CHANGED THAT SUMMER. Out of an abrupt and ragged end to childhood I took my first steps into a magnificent landscape, and it embraced me, a motherless teenage girl who needed something to believe in again. The Rocky Mountain ranges, the solidity of the ground, and the honest responses from the trout supported my first attempts to reestablish trust between me and the world. From that time on, Montana always called me back.

And so I grew up. I attended the Castilleja School in Palo Alto, California, then went to Vassar College. After gradua-

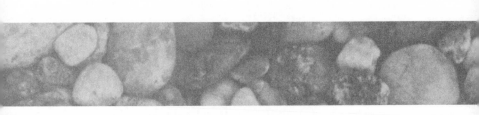

tion, and before what I assumed would be a career of some kind in a major city, I decided I needed to "take some time off" and moved to Bozeman. My first full-time job was as a copywriter and announcer at a radio station. While my college friends attended law school, or took their master's degrees, or started careers in New York, Boston, or Los Angeles, I found my place in what appeared to be the middle of nowhere.

I thrived that first winter, despite subzero temperatures and the biggest snowstorm in a decade. Adjusting to a Montana winter meant plugging in my car to keep the engine warm, wearing Sorrels (insulated rubber-soled boots) and thick wool socks, and learning to ski. While the rest of the country complained about snow, Bozeman couldn't wait for it to arrive. When it came, a blue light atop the highest building downtown started flashing, alerting skiers that fresh powder was falling. You could almost hear the cheers.

During thaws I fished the spring creeks in Livingston, and when summer finally arrived my weekends were spent fly fishing the Gallatin, the Madison, and Yellowstone Park. I was usually alone, talking to the water and the fish, feeling my way around rivers and landscape. Before I knew it, a year had passed, and then another, and then another. Montana had become my home. Concerned that I should have some kind of social life, friends arranged to have me meet a man whose affection for the outdoors and for fly fishing seemed to match mine.

Within a year, Royal Wulffs attached to long wire stems were tucked into my wedding bouquet, and I was married. I was happy to have found someone to share my life for reasons I believed were lasting and true. Together we opened a fly shop, a dream we both thought would fulfill us. And it did—for a while.

He was the first person I knew who organized his fishing gear. My fishing gear etiquette amounted to tossing rods willy-nilly into the back of the car, to be untangled and sorted out later. Fly boxes that had fallen in the water were never opened to dry out, but left shut in vest pockets, the contents rusting quietly in the darkness. I paid no attention to organizing fly patterns by size or species or type; #14 caddis patterns were stabbed next to #6 woolly buggers, which in turn were next to #18 parachute Adams. Fly fishing at my father's elbow had taught me that the act of fishing was everything, and everything else, including all the necessary paraphernalia, was not to be taken seriously. I was trained to look for rises, boulders, seam lines, dark waters, and then use all my craft and stealth to get a fly before a trout's hungry eyes.

My casual attitude toward expensive fly rods and flies brought my husband's palm to his forehead; he rolled his eyes in exasperation almost every time we went fishing together. I felt like a child when he spoke to me about how I managed my gear. I couldn't understand how anyone could expend so much energy caring about fishing tackle. Back in our fly shop, he kept hook packets and fly-tying materials neatly organized on the pegboards. The fly bins were enormous; there were several hundred patterns to choose from. After customers had picked over the flies, my husband would retrace their steps, poke his finger into the bins, and push the flies around so that the right fly was in the right bin. If someone leaned over the counter and left a smudge, he spritzed the glass with Windex as soon as they had left. The misalignment of packets on the pegboard never bothered me; and I figured the flies in the bin would eventually get mixed up anyway; and who cared about smudges on the glass.

He did the ordering, most of the selling, and kept track of the books. I was confident that his years of experience in fly-fishing retail before our marriage meant he knew what he was doing, but if I suggested we run more ads, he told me the shop couldn't afford it. If I thought we needed better signage, he told me that it was fine as it was. If I turned the heat up on the thermostat, he quietly walked over and turned it back down.

We started to have difficulty connecting outside our fly shop as well. After going to a movie I'd ask him, "So what did you think about it?" and he'd say—"It was good." I would continue, "Yeah, but what did you like about it?" and he would answer, "I don't know. It was a movie. I liked it. What more do you want me to say?" I'd grit my teeth, open the trunk in the basement of my consciousness where I stored all the things that were wrong with us, toss the incident in, and slam the lid shut. I filled that trunk full, then went out and got another one.

My husband was a good fisher and knew what patterns were working on which river. I figured you had to be there to really know. No prescription worked for every river at every time of the day or even within the same hour of the same day. I knew some idea was better than no idea, but would stammer when it came to making declarative statements about which fly went with which river, as if we were matching shoes and belts. Some clients seemed uncomfortable with my age and my gender, interpreting both as indicating a lack of experience. They seemed worried by my seemingly vague responses; what they wanted was a recitation of simple facts. Eventually they would ask for my husband, or wait for him to finish talking with another customer.

I learned to be more assertive about delivering fishing information until, like a waitress reciting the day's specials, I could say such things as "Caddis are coming off the Madison on the lower sections. Elk-hair caddis, sizes fourteen and sixteen being the best producers. Reports from the Gallatin are good near Big Sky, with attractor patterns and gold-bead nymphs working best. Yellowstone is still colored and isn't expected to clear for another week."

I dreaded certain customers, the ones who would come in and talk for an hour or more about what they had talked about the last time they had come in, which was what they had talked about the time before that. Their favorite topic, of course, was where they had caught a fish and what they had used. Then they tried to engage me in conversation, asking if I had fished this or that river and used this or that fly. It felt as if there were a relay team of these people tagging each other outside the door as one replaced the other.

The only relief I got was when a customer became serious about buying a fly rod. That meant I could take him outside to cast, escaping from the store and getting away from the constant patter about the good old days on local rivers, and how now it was ruined by yuppies, out-of-staters, and other idiots. My success at selling rods came as a result of my natural interest in fly casting. I discovered I had a knack for teaching. Soon I was giving a casting lesson every time I sold a rod, which was more and more often.

To add to our income, I developed fly-casting and fly-fishing programs. I also apprenticed as a guide, passed the state exam as a licensed Montana outfitter, and started a guide business. Then one October I discovered why I had been feeling nauseated and dizzy for over a month. We were going to have a baby.

Complications during the last two months of my pregnancy kept me out of the store, off any river, and flat on my back. Our son arrived on time, but I had no idea how exhausted a new baby could make its mother. I thought that because I was young and strong and healthy I would be like a woman in a rice paddy: I'd be back at work immediately with my baby strapped to my back. But that summer my husband handled the store mostly by himself. His resentment started to build. He was getting tired of working alone. I was plain tired. Our son was colicky; his crying had stripped my nerves of their myelin by dinnertime. My husband would arrive from a disappointing day of sales and, as I spooned mashed potatoes and pork chops onto his plate, tell me that I had to do more to help him.

On the days I minded the store, I brought the baby with me. Nursing a baby while giving a customer a river report or suggesting fly patterns took its toll. We hired someone part-time, but he left when fall arrived and the season slowed. My husband announced that he was quitting the store. He said he was fed up with slow sales, felt abandoned by me, and wanted us to move to another town. I thought we could diversify inventory, find a better location—anything but close the door on our dreams. Other couples made lives together as fly fishers and shop owners. Why couldn't we? He blamed me. I blamed him. The baby cried.

We closed the store. My husband went back to work at a former employer's. I stayed home with our son, but planned to continue offering fly-fishing courses, casting lessons, and guide services. For three long winters we struggled with our relationship and spent hours in a counselor's office. We promised each other we would try to keep an eye on the bigger picture, try harder to accept each other's faults, and try to remember why we had fallen in love in the first place. During the summers I found a full-time sitter for my son and I stepped back into the landscape that had healed my wounded soul before, only this time as a guide I led others to its waters. My heart soared with joy when one of my clients, immersed in a cool summer river, holding trout for the first time, looked up at me astonished. I knew the feeling so well. And yet when I stood under Montana's big sky looking for new inspiration, she seemed to be irritated, asking, *What? What more do you want?* I was afraid to ask for more, but when I drove home, I'd circle the block dreading another evening with my troubled marriage.

———

THAT WAS THE WORLD into which Lars Olsson's voice, calling from Sweden, came in over the answering machine.

"... I understand it is too late to have a fly-fishing school this year, but perhaps you could come over and have a look at the river and see what you think, if it's the right place for future schools. Also, I wish to invite you, along with two British journalists, to visit a fishing camp in Lapland, which will be part of a package we are trying to create between my river and the camp. I would like to speak with you about this, so please call me back. My number is ..."

Adventure suddenly loomed before me—a new landscape, a new river. My hand hovered over the phone, hesitating, but before Lars Olsson could hang up I answered,

"Hello," I said. "This is Jennifer."

Water Music

GUIDE TRIPS WERE RESCHEDULED so that I could travel to Sweden in August. At the library I studied an atlas, but Lars Olsson's little village of Gimdalen—was too small to appear on any map. The only book about Sweden I found was hilariously out of date; it led you to believe the country was populated entirely by peasants in folk dress, perpetually dancing around some sort of Maypole. The travel guides focused on sight-seeing in Stockholm; there was nothing about the forest country where I would be traveling. It was all so mysterious, I smiled and closed the books. I would just let it happen. See where it took me.

As the plane descended into the Scandinavian morning, I could see red-and-white farmhouses next to neatly squared grain and potato fields. I had arrived in Sweden.

The first thing that struck me was how quiet people were. The loudest noise in the terminal came from the sound of shoes clicking on the linoleum as we all headed toward customs. After clearing customs and gathering up my bags, I was directed to the domestic terminal a five-minute walk away. Again, despite the crowd of business travelers dragging luggage on wheels and pressing cell phones to their ears, the atmosphere was calm. No gesticulating of hands, or loud conversation, or sharp elbows. The announcements over the public-address system were introduced with a pleasant three-note chime followed by a soothing voice. For anyone used to hearing bored discount-store employees demanding price checks, this lack of audio abuse was appreciated. It was so quiet I was able to nap at the gate during the two-hour wait for the flight to the city of Östersund, the fourth and last leg of my journey.

The flight to Östersund gave me the chance to see southern Sweden from the air. Ireland may be the greenest place in the world, but Sweden must come in a close second. I had yet to see any evidence of a freeway or high-rise. It seemed to me that Sweden was a sea of forests, lakes, and farmland sailed by those sturdy rectangular red-and-white farmhouses and outbuildings. I felt at ease. If nothing else, I understood trees and water and blue sky.

After landing I waited while the rows of people in front

of me emptied into the aisle. Tired from twenty-four hours of travel, I sighed. I hoped I had made the right decision. Weeks before this trip took place I had made several inquiries via friends in the fishing business to find out if Lars Olsson had spent any time in jail for doing harm to foreign fishing guides. I had been assured that his record was clean, and that he and his wife would be excellent hosts. Nonetheless, I intended to be on the alert. Gathering myself, my fly rods, and my thoughts, I stepped off the plane to meet the voice.

A man in his forties, of medium height, with gray hair, blue eyes, and an athletic physique, greeted me with a warm smile. He was as friendly looking as his voice had promised.

"You are brave to come all this way," he said, shaking my hand.

"Yes," I agreed, "it's a long way."

Firs lined the road on the way to Gimdalen. Here and there, quaint-looking summer cottages with dark windows peeked out at the road like curious old ladies. Spooked by our passing, a capercaillie, the largest grouse in the world, comparable in size to the American wild turkey, flew from its perch nearby and disappeared like smoke into the deep green woods. A reindeer that had strayed from its Sami— indigenous Scandinavian people—owner during the winter was spotted grazing uneasily in the shadows. Lars asked me to be on the lookout for moose, which could dash unexpectedly in front of the car. That was a common occurrence in this part of the world.

After an hour's drive we arrived at the concrete-and-steel bridge that marked the beginning of Idsjöströmmen—the one-mile section of the sixty-mile-long Gim River that Lars leased and managed. I stepped from the car to admire the river. I knelt and dipped my hand into its waters. Idsjöströmmen reminded me of the Gallatin River in Montana; it had the same width and the same rounded boulders; trees and brush grew along the banks. Immediately I recognized thresholds, pools, and runs where fish most likely held. I could already see where I would wade and cast. It seemed pristine. Had I not already known that this section of river had been restored from its former life as a logging channel I would never have guessed it.

Yet for over a hundred and fifty years, Idsjöströmmen did have another life, as a timber highway. The Gim River is only one of many rivers that wind their way from the Scandinavian mountains to the Baltic. In the mid-1800s, when Sweden began logging her forests in earnest, harvested logs needed to be transported to the Baltic mills for processing and exportation. Sweden's lakes and waterways were the obvious routes, and by the hundreds of thousands, logs were hauled to the numerous lakes and rivers to be set afloat for the journey downstream. To create the smooth deep channel necessary for the timber to pass through easily, the riverbeds had been blown free of boulders and obstructions by Alfred Nobel's dynamite. Stone retaining walls had been erected, and floating walkways anchored for men to guide the logs from. Almost everyone in the forests worked for the timber companies; generations lived off the economic base they provided.

During the 1970s it became more economical to haul the timber off in trucks. The timber companies completely abandoned the river system for transporting logs. An era of logging that had required intense manual labor finally ended and the last of a long line of people who made their living in the forest were left behind as well.

However, the forest companies were required by law to remove the retaining walls, dams, walkways, and other structures that had been built to facilitate the transportation of timber. Some of what they promised to do they did, but the effort was mostly limited to the removal of man-made structures, and even many of those were left in place. This meant that spring runoff and summer flows flushed through, scouring the riverbeds and leaving the rivers barely habitable for aquatic insect life. Without an abundant food source, breaks in the current, or deep pools in which to escape predators and warm temperatures, grayling and brown trout struggled to survive in this harsh new environment. Fishermen kept almost everything they caught, depleting the resource even further.

In the mid-seventies, Lars, and his wife, Margit, returned to visit her family home in Gimdalen. As teachers they had the summers off, and Lars took advantage of the time to explore and fish nearby Idsjöströmmen. Even with the wounds the fishery had suffered from being dynamited and overfished, he was able to catch wild grayling. This was particularly impressive since acid rain was devastating other fisheries in Sweden at a growing rate. In this regard what set Idsjöströmmen apart from other Swedish rivers was that it benefited from a good amount of natural limestone in the area and in the streambed. The limestone kept the pH in the water near an optimal level of 8.1, increasing the trout and graylings' chances for survival. In addition, Idsjöströmmen was located at the mouth of Idsjön, a lake which is six miles long and nearly two miles wide, and borders the western side of Gimdalen. During the late fall grayling migrate to Idsjön and winter in its temperature-stable depths until spring, when they return to spawn then summer in the river.

Because of these advantages, Lars and other fly fishermen believed Idsjöströmmen was still viable, though they also knew that more work would be necessary to help the river reach its full potential. Together they formed an organization and called themselves the Gim River Environmental Group (Gimåns Miljögrupp). Along with the Gimdalen Fishing Right Owners and the County Administration Board of Jämtland, Lars and his organization joined in the effort to finish what the timber industry had only started to do—return the riverbed to the way it had been before being manipulated for logs. An excavator was hired to lift and tear down the last of the logging structures. The stone retaining walls were completely dismantled. Pools were scooped out to create protected places for the grayling to hold. Boulders and large stones were arranged to create oxygen-generating runs and riffles. Idsjöströmmen's transformation was, as I could now see, astonishing. It looked natural and untouched.

In 1981, having until then spent summers in Gimdalen with Margit's family since the early seventies, Lars, his wife, and their young twin sons, Magnus and Fredrik, moved back to the village to live year-round. They continued teaching in nearby communities. Lars waited eagerly for the river restoration to show an increase in the number and size of grayling. The environment they had created was perfect. There were places for the grayling to spawn, rest, and feed. But after observing this experiment for nearly twelve years, however, Lars became convinced that the bottomless bag limit still being permitted was the reason grayling were not yet thriving and populating the river.

In 1988 Gimdalen's fishing board (essentially consisting of landowners) approached Lars with a new plan. In the best interests of the river and the area, they told him, they had decided to lease him the fishing rights for a fee, but only if he continued with plans to develop the river as a public recreational fishery. They wanted to test his idea of creating and managing an environmentally friendly business with the potential of providing the village with a renewable industry. It was the first time this kind of arrangement had been made in Sweden.

So began the next phase of Idsjöströmmen's new life. Lars decided to limit the number of fishers per day and restrict fishing to fly fishing with barbless hooks and catch-and-release only. It was his prescription for Idsjöströmmen's final and enduring recovery.

Lars knelt beside me and scooped water from the river with a carved wooden cup he had brought from the car.

"Here. Drink this," he said.

I hesitated. I had been conditioned never to drink the water from the rivers I fished in Montana. If the Giardia parasite or amebic dysentery didn't get you, the fertilizer and pesticide runoff might. I shook my head.

"There's nothing dangerous in the water. You can't get sick," Lars promised as he held up the cup of water.

It was the first time I ever drank water directly from a river. The water was cool and fresh.

The entrance to the village was at the crest of a hill. Red-and-white–trimmed houses came immediately into view. I had learned that the burgundy-red paint of almost every house, cottage, and barn in the country is called *falu röd,* or "Falun Red." Lars explained that Falun was the name of a town where in the 1800s copper mining had boomed. A byproduct of copper extraction was a reddish powder called *koppar vitrol,* and from it inexpensive paint could be made by combining it with linseed oil. The low cost, the added protection it gave to wood siding, and the attractive effects have made it nearly universal in Sweden.

However, I was also assured that *falu röd* was not the only color you could consider for the exterior of your house. At the hardware store you had the luxury of choosing from about five other colors. There didn't seem to be a law preventing the Swedes from painting their houses, say, pink, but out of respect for tradition and neighbors, brushes do not dip into anything that might attract unnecessary attention. American homeowners are used to feeling they can do whatever they want with their houses. Yet here was one less thing to fuss over, one less decision that had to be made. You could never go wrong if you painted your house *falu röd.* Other, perhaps more important concerns, could then be given the attention they deserved. I wondered how else life could be simplified by reducing choice.

Lars told me that Gimdalen was one of hundreds of small domestic "islands" in Sweden's forest country. Loosely translated, *Gimdalen* means "In the valley of the Gim River." Nearly a hundred people live within its boundaries. Most villagers are retirees; others work for the local township of Bräcke, for the timber company, or as teachers or secretaries. A single road connects Gimdalen to the outside world. It runs through the middle of the settlement like a zipper. A person would probably not come to the village unless he or she lived there, knew someone who lived there, delivered the mail, hauled timber, wanted to fish Idsjöströmmen, or had gotten lost.

Human history in Gimdalen is over seven thousand years

old. Graves dating from the Iron Age are marked; their distinctive circular formation can be found near Idsjön. During the Middle Ages, Gimdalen was on the route traveled by pilgrims visiting churches and holy relics in Trondheim, Norway. It has been suggested that originally *Gimdalen* meant "the going-through place," a name given to it by the pilgrims who found safe passage on their way to Trondheim.

In any event, the village was formally established in 1757. Enveloped by the beauty of the fir, pine, and birch forest landscape, villagers lived by hunting, fishing, and berry picking. They also farmed potatoes, planted rye and barley, and raised cows, chickens, and pigs. Between the early 1800s and mid-1900s the focus shifted from farming to logging. Many families found they could live comfortably by selling the timber on their land, or by signing on as one of the laborers who felled, floated, or milled timber for forest companies. After World War II, modern machinery and new timber-harvesting techniques began replacing manual labor. This was the beginning of the end of the logging industry as people in the forest country had known it to be. The forest country started losing its younger generations to the major cities on the coast and to the south, where there was work. Grand houses that once had sheltered generations of families within their thick timbered walls became empty and now slumped, as if from the weight of age and the accumulated years of neglect. I found it hard to believe that Gimdalen had once been a thriving community with not one but two grocery stores, a post office, bakery, grammar school, and ski factory.

Lars parked in front of Kullagården, the largest building in the village, a three-story schoolhouse that had been converted to serve as a community center with rooms to rent.

Carrying my bags, he led me up the stairs to the second story and pushed the door open to a small but tidy room with windows that looked out over a waist-high field of rye. Against one wall were a side table and a bunk bed. The bath and shower were down the hall. The two British journalists, Nick and John, had arrived earlier and were waiting to meet us at a nearby farm where Tora, Lars's mother-in-law, was literally up to her elbows in dough, baking traditional Swedish *tunnbröd*.

After dropping off the luggage, Lars and I walked up the dirt road past Kullagården to the highest knoll of the village, where Tora's farm was situated. Passing through the courtyard we arrived in front of a *falu-röd*–colored two-story rectangular building. Smoke from its chimney curled leisurely upward into the cloudless sky. Wooden steps leading to the narrow covered porch were worn from over a hundred years of use. A set of large dark-green double doors with burgundy trim led into a hallway. On the left were a storage room and a set of stairs leading to the second story. Directly ahead was a cozy little room, complete with fireplace and a wooden sofa. And to my right was the doorway to the baking cottage. Tora looked up at us and smiled.

In her early seventies, Tora was of medium build and height, and wore a red-and-white–checked pinafore apron over her long-sleeved dress. Her hair was covered by a clean muslin kerchief. Her hands were dusted with flour, as was a spot on her cheek where she had brushed it with her hand. She greeted Lars and they began to converse.

Most farms have a baking cottage. Essentially this consists of a clean, dry room with a large brick oven. In the center of the room are one or two birch tables the length and width of twin-sized beds. The tables have a knotless surface sanded to the smoothness of glass so the bread dough does not stick when it is being kneaded or rolled flat into large thin circular shapes that remind me of jumbo-sized tortillas.

Built specifically to bake *tunnbröd,* the oven is a familiar and much-loved fixture of rural Sweden. It has a recessed brick shelf capped by a low-domed brick ceiling, which captures the heat from the fire and holds it. The heat becomes intense, which is why the oven inhabits a separate room.

I was introduced to Tora, whose kind eyes and sweet grandmotherly face were very welcoming. Across the room were the two British journalists. They stood up and we made introductions all around. John was well known in England for his books on brown trout and grayling fishing; Nick worked as a journalist for various fishing publications.

Tora had been in the cottage since five o'clock that morning. We witnessed her roll out and bake the last of the *tunnbröds.* Then Lars produced wine and cheese to go with a sampling of Tora's fresh bread, and in the room's timeless atmosphere we started to get acquainted. Being fly fishers on a fly-fishing adventure, we quickly turned the conversation to tackle preferences and favorite rivers. I sensed that before long we would be great friends.

The next day we geared up for a first attempt on Idsjöströmmen. One wonderful thing about fishing with other experienced fly fishers is that they know how to take care of themselves. Having been a fishing guide for so long, I had almost forgotten what fishing without a dependent felt like. I could look at the water and decide what fly to use based on what I wanted rather than on what I thought the clients could handle. Most beginning fly fishers cannot see small fly patterns or fish with certain types of flies, such as "emergers," with any confidence or skill. The pressure to get clients to where the fish are, and in a hurry, sometimes means I have to tie on gold-bead patterns for quick results.

A gold-bead fly is what its name says: a metallic, gold-colored bead that gets threaded onto the hook and pushed up next to the hook-eye. Fur and feathers are then tied to the shank. Successful flies, such as hare's ears or prince nymphs, have recently been redressed as gold-bead hare's ear and gold-bead prince nymphs. Although gold beads are very effective, using them made me feel a little guilty. Once a fly has been augmented with metal it seems to slip out of the fly-fishing category. Gold beads attract fish the same way a spinning lure does, by flashing in the water sparking the fish's curiosity. I like classic patterns—soft hackles, wet flies, delicate dries—and using classic techniques to stimulate takes. For most people the goal of fishing is to catch fish, but when you have been a fly fisher as long as I have you can get a little strange. You make up rules for your fishing, a sort of self-imposed obstacle course.

In the middle of my fishing preparations I noticed that both John and Nick had tied on gold-bead patterns. Lars suddenly asked what I was going to fish with. All three men turned to look at me. It felt like a trap. I thought that maybe I was wrong about gold beads. After all, I didn't really have any idea what a Swedish grayling would take. I studied my fly box as if considering what to fish with for the first time in my life. Lars stepped over to see what kind of flies I had. "Use this one," he said as he reached for a #16 parachute Adams and then dropped it into the palm of my hand. I know he was only being helpful, but I didn't want to be seen as needing help. I tied on my fly. The group dispersed with cheerful farewells and wishes for good fishing.

I walked the trail downstream. The Englishmen worked over two deep pools upstream. Suddenly John had a fish. Lars appeared from the bank to photograph him. I watched the men. They seemed so absorbed. I suddenly missed my son intensely. I would be away from him for almost two weeks. What on earth was I doing here?

Come on, I told myself, *get it together.*

Moving toward the river's edge, I closed my eyes. There's nothing better than the sound of water to drown out all other sounds, especially the ones produced when thoughts run together too fast. A river can be loud and yet still help a person to concentrate. When I opened my eyes, I knew I was not in my home waters, where sagebrush flats fill the valleys and craggy mountains tower overhead, but like music, a river can be read, and looking at Idsjöströmmen that first time, I knew I could learn to play it.

I waded toward a line of rocks where the current spilled smoothly over their rounded tops before rushing into a pool beneath them. The places that looked most promising to me were the area just above the line of rocks, where fish can be counted on to take aquatic foods, and the seam line of riffled water at the edges of the pool in front of me. Fish take food in places where the current is choppy; the broken surface affords them protection from predators, and the churning water carries helpless aquatic insects, such as caddis larvae and mayfly nymphs. All a trout or grayling need do is wait for something to float by. I decided to go for the riffled water.

Three casts and I saw the splash of a fish taking. What I

also saw was a flash of burgundy color before the fly and the grayling tucked under the surface. I had met my first grayling.

Fishing friends had warned me before I'd left that I might find grayling disappointing. To them, what made a game fish exciting was how hard it fought, how big it was, and how many times it jumped. I agree. A wild rainbow trout is about the most exciting cold-water fish to catch. It jumps and runs and makes a lot of satisfying commotion before you get a chance to net it. And when you get it to hand, it treats you to a sight as mysterious and fine as a sunrise—great red and pink slashes along its spotted sides. Brown trout can be about as terrifying, especially the big ones in the two-pound-and-up category. They do not always jump, but are known to point themselves away from you and move to warp speed. Grayling are more like the cutthroat trout found in Yellowstone Park. Often after they grab the fly they pull violently during the first few runs, then go deep and try to stay there.

My first grayling did exactly that. It ran, it tugged, it tried to dodge me. I played it carefully, waded after it, and, once I had it in the net, I took a good look. The grayling had the most amazing burgundy-and-blue-green–colored dorsal fin, something trout don't have. In fact, the colorful dorsal fin is the grayling's most attractive feature. I returned my prize to the river and watched it dart away from my shadow.

Returning to the line of rock, I placed the parachute Adams back in the riffle to see if there were other grayling interested in some exercise. Several more went for a run with me at the other end. I happily followed. The men remained upstream; I was in my own world downstream. Two hours later, Lars called to me from the bank to say that lunch was ready at the campfire near the first windbreak. I reeled up and simply stood in Idsjöströmmen's fresh, clean current, listening to it tumble past on its way to the Baltic. The notion that this sound might become like a favorite song, one that I would want to hear over and over again, had not yet occurred to me. It soon would.

The Rock

FISHING LARS'S NEWLY RESTORED RIVER for wild grayling, then being invited to swoop over the Arctic tundra by helicopter and land in Swedish Lapland at a remote camp where reindeer grazed in the distance, was just the thing for an adventure-starved outdoorswoman. The helicopter slowly rose, lifting Lars, John, Nick, and me over the Kiruna Airport, then accelerated toward the vast Arctic wilderness to the northwest.

None of us had ever flown in a helicopter before. The noise from the propeller was so loud, we all had to wear headphones with small microphones attached to protect our hearing and to communicate. The others chatted away. I observed the landscape below.

For half an hour we flew over the almost treeless tundra a hundred and fifty miles north of the Arctic Circle on our way to the Tjuonajokk Fishing Camp. Because the winter lasts for over nine months, the birch trees, shrubs, and berries that grow there are dwarfed; they look like bonsai. The open space and rolling hills reminded me of the American prairie. Trails crossed the land in a variety of places; these were the ancient migration paths of reindeer. Each year, guided by instinct, the reindeer find their way to the heights of their traditional summer grazing lands, then migrate back down again when the season turns to winter. Winter never seems far off, for in the distance glacial fields and snow bowls mark the Scandinavian mountains year-round.

Sloping hills rose up along our flight path. At one point our pilot climbed the face of a rather high rocky ridge; we could almost touch the enormous round boulders that glaciers had left behind millions of years before. After the helicopter crested the top, the land suddenly disappeared from beneath us, and the aircraft roared down the cliff face on the other side. For a moment I thought my soul had separated from its earthly mooring. My head became light with the sensation of floating. I gripped the seat. All of us, except the pilot, let out a collective whoop of surprise. Realizing we had just been treated to a bit of passive-aggressive pilot fun, we expressed our relief at surviving it with laughter.

Minutes later, Tjuonajokk came into view. The staff was there to greet us as we gently touched down next to the main lodge. The camp is only accessible by air, foot, or boat and is situated on the north bank of the Kaitum River, a tributary of the Kalix River, whose headwaters begin high in the Scandinavian mountains. It is part of one of the longest undammed river systems in Sweden.

People come during the ten-week season of this northerly outpost to fish for grayling, char, and brown trout. Rustic cabins outfitted with bunk beds provide rooms for over fifty guests; the toilets are a row of outhouses. Propane and solar power are used for heating; guests bathe in the sauna down by the boat dock. The main lodge houses the dining room, general store, and a large sitting room with a massive stone fireplace. After dinner, guests gather on the couches and chairs in front of the fire and stare into it intensely.

The camp was designed with the rugged outdoorsman in mind, but there is a resident chef well known for his gourmet meals. Regional specialties include mushrooms and berries picked right outside the back door of the lodge. Our first evening, we were treated to reindeer filet with lingonberry sauce, boiled potatoes, sautéed mushrooms, fresh-baked bread still warm from the oven, followed by cloudberries (so called because of their slightly puffy appearance) and cream. After that we waddled back to our rooms for a good night's sleep.

Each day, after a hearty breakfast, we marched to the dock, where we hopped into our assigned boats and motored downstream or upstream, depending on the recommendations made by Lars and the Tjuonajokk guide assigned to us. In the evenings, since the sun never sets during the summers in Lapland, we ventured out after dinner sometimes as late as midnight. Guests could fish twenty-four hours a day if they liked; boats could be heard on the river at almost any hour.

Lars was a generous host, making sure that we were comfortable and had everything we needed. He treated John and Nick like brothers, and they in turn treated me like a sister. John and Nick made fun of the way I held my fork and mashed down my potatoes; I made fun of how overly polite they were about who should get out of the boat first; and all three of us made fun of Lars and how laden his fishing vest was with gadgets.

So when was it that I noticed Lars noticing me? Was it when I waded out into the icy current of the Kaitum and he immediately followed and insisted I use his wading staff? Was it when his eyes went from intense focus to sparkling with laughter at something I said? Was it because he took the time to ask me questions, and then really listened to my answers? When did I finally understand that he wanted my attention exclusively?

Sometimes, at night, when I hear suspicious sounds, I listen, barely breathing, waiting for the sound to make sense, to reveal its source. Not knowing whether it is an intruder or something benign, such as branches blowing against the side of the house, I remain motionless, paralyzed, until the blood pulsing in my ears becomes deafening, making it impossible to hear anything else. I get out of bed and go investigate, only to find that it is nothing more than the icemaker dropping ice cubes, or the house creaking from a change in temperature.

Something about Lars made me feel *that* awake and aware. Something bewildering was happening, and I couldn't identify what it was. I wanted to get to know him better and at the same time didn't want to get too close. I liked talking to him. I found his insights and knowledge appealing. He was genuinely warm and kind and always considerate of others, so I assumed that he was like that with everyone; I was not singled out for special attention. I did not want to have feelings I could not afford, but there were times when I wished Nick and John would go to bed early, or go fishing on their own, so that I could be alone with Lars. Then I became afraid again.

At the dock on the last day of our stay, Lars took my fishing gear and life vest and placed them in the bow of his boat. Nick, John, and the guide filed into the boat next to ours. They went in one direction. Lars steered our boat in the other. I tried to tell myself that there was no need to panic. It was just a fishing trip and I was a fisher; all I needed to think about was fishing. When we landed on the bank below Tjirtjam Rapids—there were reports of large grayling being caught here—I helped Lars pull the boat up and then quickly set about finding a place to fish in solitude. Parting with what I had intended to be a carefree wave, I hiked downstream.

The rocks that lined the bottom of the Kaitum were large and unstable. I stepped out onto a boulder that I thought felt secure and solid, but as soon as both my feet were in place it began to wobble. It took some shifting and shuffling to steady myself before I could begin to cast.

I didn't see the fish take my fly; I simply knew it was there. A fisher experiences moments of knowing, without being able to explain how, that the fish should strike. An inner sense sends a message to the arm to lift the rod tip and connect. So I did. A large, steely grayling, fortified by a life in the Arctic current of the Kaitum, pulled at me, as if to draw me in. It fought hard. I lost my footing on the seesawing rock, tripped, and felt the power of the river trying to push me down. I managed to keep from falling in and waded back to quieter water near shore where I could get hold of my gray-ling before releasing it. Its strong thick body writhed and twisted in my hand, insisting on being set free.

Since the beginning of the trip, the beauty of the grayling's dorsal fin had become a great discovery for me. I grew more and more enchanted with each grayling I caught, and could feel my prejudice against it for not being a trout slipping away. It was getting easier to let the grayling be a friend. I held my fish in the water until it surged back to life in the river.

A large rock warmed by the sun beckoned me upstream. The near tumble into the river had given me reason to take a break. I climbed up onto the rock and sat cross-legged, eyes closed, soaking up the warmth of the Lapland sun.

I heard rather than saw him approach. When I opened my eyes, Lars was standing next to me. He seemed lost. He had come across as a natural leader, someone who always seemed to know what was going to happen next—but not as he stood quietly beside me. The silence grew. I knew without know-ing. He leaned forward and brushed his lips against my cheek. I could feel him trembling.

"I hope you're not upset. I just had to ... I ..."

"It's okay," I stammered, looking at him earnestly and helplessly at the same time.

"I just want to be near you. I don't want to frighten you. I don't mean to ask for anything more. I just like being around you," he said.

"I like that you like being around me."

Lars brightened and then backed away.

"Where are you going?" I asked.

"I have to leave. I'll come back and fish with you after a while. I just had to have my answer, and now I have it."

He turned to leave. Then he turned back again.

"Thank you. Thank you for making me so happy."

I watched him walk upstream and step into the river. I felt something inside loosen and float above the Arctic tundra. I let the pulse of the river pounding in my heart bring me back to that place at the top of the world. I held on to the rock and watched the man who made me feel this way cast for beautiful grayling, and hoped that he would never wade out of sight.

New Favorite Nation

THE AIR IN BOZEMAN smelled of summer—cut grass, barbecue, rain on warm dry fields—as I stepped off the plane. When I held and kissed my son, the scent of baby shampoo in his hair melted my mother's heart. I smiled at my husband, and for an instant I almost forgot where I had been and whom I had met and what I had felt. I walked to the car in the parking lot and back toward my regularly scheduled life.

In the beginning, Lars called me once a week. We talked as comfortably as two old friends about our mornings and afternoons, or what we had planned for the guiding and fly-

fishing season ahead. He had been a schoolteacher and listened easily while I told him about Peter's triumphant first day at preschool, and about my tears after dropping him off. Lars encouraged me to pursue my interest in writing and speaking engagements. His confidence in me was greater than my own; I found I needed to talk to him more than just once a week. Soon we spoke to each other twice a week, then every day, then twice a day, then whenever we felt like it.

The phone company knew something was up before my husband did. One evening when I was out, my husband answered the phone and an AT&T representative informed him that their records showed a high volume of international calls to Sweden and wondered if we might be interested in applying for the "Favorite Nation" discount.

"Have you been making a lot of calls to Sweden?" my husband asked.

"Sweden?"

"Yeah. The phone company says we have a lot of calls to Sweden."

"Well, like how many?"

"I don't know. Maybe you should talk to them."

So I called AT&T and ordered the special discount on my new favorite nation and made sure I got to the mail first each day. Sometimes when I called, Lars's wife answered. My lowest moment was hanging up on her without saying anything. I felt like a criminal. Margit was a good person. She and I had gotten along. How could I treat her like that? Why couldn't I get a brain and leave this impossible situation alone. But when the phone rang I'd trip over rugs and crash into doorjambs in my haste to hear the click and crackle of an international call coming through the receiver.

When I wasn't sprinting for the phone, I ran red lights. I lost weight. I sang "Don't Cry for Me, Argentina" in the shower. I played Bonnie Raitt, *Something to Talk About,* at least a hundred times. I smiled more. I was in love with a man six thousand miles away, and had no plans to ever see him again, but I carried on as if we were going to have dinner together that very evening. None of it seemed real, but it fed my loneliness.

We wrote long letters. Lars described mallards in flight, the chill in the air, the colors of fall. He spoke about his river, his missing us. I wrote back about my day, how I read my son to sleep at night, how I missed the smell of a birch-wood campfire, and his smile. Lars wrote about how the days were getting shorter, the nights longer, and how preparations for the red-hatted Christmas *tomtens* (Santas) were under way. I called to wish him a Happy New Year. Sometimes our letters burned with desire, and we didn't trust those feelings to the fax or to the mail, so we wrote them on our computers, read them to each other over the phone, then hit the delete button.

I lived parallel lives: the one that met me in the mirror, the other in my imagination, on the phone, and in letters. Which was real—Monday mornings, teaching my son to tie his shoes, and having a man to hold at the end of the day; or was it the warmth and wisdom and affection magically transmitted to me over thousands of miles via satellite, via cable, via some peculiar electronic pulse that refused to get lost in the darkness of space? After all, did writing letters and talking over the phone fit the definition of an affair? Maybe we were only friends.

My irritation with my husband proved otherwise. He couldn't understand my dissatisfaction with our relationship.

He was doing his part, why couldn't I play mine? Back in the counselor's office I tattled on my husband's behavior, trying in my curiously twisted way to get him to fix everything, thinking, *If you would just, if you would only, if you could, then I wouldn't have gotten me into this jam!*

Oddly enough, it was a huge relief when I finally got caught. Lars was traveling in England and left a message on the answering machine. Maybe he said "darling" instead of my name—I can't remember—but my husband heard something in the voice that made him understand, and he confronted me.

"I know what's going on," he said.

"What's going on?" I replied, knowing exactly where the conversation was headed.

"I know why you've been acting so strangely."

"Really, why?"

"There's something going on between you and Lars."

The person least likely to have a clue was the first to say what was going on out loud. I wanted the deceit to end; I wanted to get rid of my mystery life and bring it out in the open where I could let it be real.

"Yes. You're right," I answered.

"I'm getting a lawyer," he said as he left the room.

"I'm getting one too," I shouted after him.

And so we drew our lines.

In *The Sound of Music,* Maria went to the hills; in *Gone With the Wind,* Scarlet got her strength from Tara. I went to Hylite Creek, located just south of town, and sat on a boulder watching the water tumble past. Why had I held on to a marriage that had distorted me? I was disgusted at how easily I had lied for months and months to cover up my feelings for

Lars—all those untruths to guard a truth. I shuddered at all the trouble my leaving would cause, and the unspeakable grief at having to watch confusion and fear cross my son's face when he heard what was going to happen to his world.

Life had taught me that lies and omissions were only temporary barriers between me and a painful, inevitable, but necessary intimacy with life and death. Something had to give. I needed to start trusting my own mind. I couldn't go on pretending for another twenty years or a day. I would have to chaperone my son through the messy world of adults and their imperfections. In exchange, he would be free to love or despise me. He would know that I was not just his mother, but a person with a life of her own, someone he could trust to tell the truth, someone he could count on to check for monsters under the bed and run them off, someone who was so scared and sad he could hear her down the hall, crying herself to sleep.

Flight

GET MARRIED AND EVERYONE smiles, crediting you
with knowing what you're doing. Get a divorce and you become a suspect at large. Divorce is the modern version of the
stocks. It only took the two of us to put our marriage together,
but it took a staff of people with doctorates in counseling and
law to get us out. Our unmatching required a court and a
judge, and we were so ill-tempered we just barely worked
out a custody agreement with the support of both our lawyers
and a mediator. Given that civil servants and paid counsel had
to listen to all the sordid details of he said/she said for hours

on end, it seems only right that they be entitled to their re-
venge: taking our depositions and asking for copies of our tax
returns.

I wasn't free to say to the judge what I wanted to say.
*Your Honor, for some time now I have been throwing care and
affection toward the wrong person, namely my husband. You see,
I know this because I met a man in Sweden, he's married and
has two teenage sons, and I've only been in his company a total
of two weeks, but we've been writing letters and calling each
other for over a year and I can tell he's the one. His wife found
out that he had feelings for me, and, well, understandably that
sort of killed the relationship for her, so she got busy and found
a boyfriend of her own and left. Now Lars is free and I'm going
to leave my marriage and we'll be together. Everything is going
to work out, so if you could just sign off on the decree I'll be on
my way.*

In effect, the court warned, *Not so fast, sister. We're going
to have a trial and put you on the stand and let the respondent's
attorney question you for numerous hours about the ownership
of assets and other financial interests including the drift boat your
husband wishes to be entitled to, and then we'll take about a
month to come up with an answer, and then your husband will
contest the decision and that will take another year or so and
you'll get bored with the whole thing and go on with your life
anyway. Just remember, you're the one who married the guy in
the first place. And don't forget you're going to create a lot of
paperwork for us in the coming months—so you just sit tight and
deal.*

My idea of waiting for a divorce was making plans for
Lars to move in as soon as possible. Three weeks after the
bedroom closet was finally free of my husband's shirts, pants,

shoes, and ties, it was scheduled to be filled up with Lars's shirts, pants, shoes, and ties. When his plane touched down on Bozeman's Gallatin Field, I felt weak. Lars stepped through the gate; I thought I was seeing a ghost. For over a year we had bounced our gazes off the light of the moon, telling ourselves that even though we couldn't see each other we were looking at the same light. Suddenly thousands of miles had shrunk to nothing and we stood looking at each other.

Though it was all so romantic, later there were moments when I wondered how this man had managed to land in my life. He also had his quirks. He believed in sleeping with the windows open when I wanted them closed. In a house full of tea bags, only loose-leaf tea would do. Like Mary Poppins, he insisted that Peter and I eat the oatmeal he cooked us for breakfast every morning, a dollop of blackberry jam on top. And to my horror, he tossed a new jar of peanut butter into the trash, calling it American junk food and banning it henceforth from the house. Meal and bedtimes were enforced. He rearranged the furniture in the living room and kitchen, and coerced me into jogging alongside him as part of a regular exercise program.

How could I have gotten free of one quirky man only to get tangled up with another? Maybe it was because he had left his home and his country and crossed an ocean for us; because he walked with Peter to school in the morning, and in the afternoon he walked him home; because he appreciated the little things in life: a beautifully shaped teapot, sharpened pencils, and birdsongs. Or because after we dared speak to each other of our fears and our vulnerabilities—even our anger (a volatile discussion resulting in the return of peanut butter to my diet) drew us closer. Maybe because one day I came into the kitchen and found Lars on his hands and knees, washing the floor. No man I knew ever scrubbed a floor—ever. He smiled and talked to me about my day while he wiped it dry.

My friends were very excited that I had acquired an exotic foreign boyfriend so soon after my separation.

"Of course, a man with a river in Sweden," they said.

But when I told them I was planning to leave the hallowed trout waters of the American West for his Swedish river during the summers, their jaws collectively dropped. Then they paused.

"Is the fishing that good there?"

"Does he have a salmon river?" some asked, hopefully.

"No," I answered, much to their disappointment. "It's a grayling and brown trout river. Mostly a grayling river. The Scandinavians and Europeans are crazy about grayling fishing," I replied, trying to make it all sound acceptable.

"He has sea-run browns, right?"

"No. Just regular brown trout. Like the ones we have here in Montana."

"What about rainbow trout? He must have rainbow trout."

"No. Rainbows are stocked fish in Sweden. This is a wild river."

Lars is seventeen years older than I am, and that drew comments as well.

"Do you think you're looking for a father figure?" a girlfriend asked directly.

"Is he having a midlife crisis?" another wanted to know.

"You know, all European men have mistresses," warned yet another.

"Will Peter go with you?" I was asked.

"Yes."

"He'll be speaking Swedish in no time. Kids pick up language just like that." They'd snap their fingers.

"Are you going to learn to speak Swedish?"

"I'm not sure."

The truth was I had not planned to, not right away at least. I wanted to be free to observe and explore without needing to be understood. I would also have the excuse of being *American*. Everyone knows Americans can't speak anything but English. And even though most Swedes speak or at least understand English, I had hoped that no one would have to feel obligated to talk to me unless they wanted to. That way I wouldn't have to answer a lot of questions.

I wondered what it would be like to remain mute while conversation flowed freely and I waited for a translation. Maybe after watching me follow Lars around like a faithful pet and stand next to him with a benign, uncomprehending smile on my face, people would think I was a bit simple.

"That socialist welfare they have there, that doesn't work, does it?" some queried.

"I don't know."

"Didn't Chernobyl blow some fallout over Sweden? The people stopped eating reindeer meat because the reindeer were grazing on radioactive grass."

"Really? I never heard that."

"They drink a lot and eat herring, right?"

"On special occasions."

"Isn't there a lot of suicide there? The people are really depressed, right?"

"I'm not sure about that. They seem more . . ."

"They're into nudity and sex, right?"

"Well, they have a healthy attitude about..."

"Sweden didn't help out in the war, did they?"

"No, but..."

"Don't you think that was kind of chicken-shit?"

"I don't know. I'm not going as the secretary of state."

To many of my acquaintances it looked as if my plan was to take my innocent child to a Communist country where drunken nudes were sad because they didn't have any wild rainbow trout to fish for.

I can't say I didn't have moments of doubt. It had taken over eight years for my guide business to grow from five trips the first summer, to over ninety trips during the last. Hundreds of miles had been driven to rivers and back again, guiding on the trout-filled waters of Montana and Yellowstone Park. I had just received a record number of bookings, and because of the pending move to Swedish fishing grounds during the fishing season I had to refer caller after caller to other capable guides. I felt the unkind reality of being dispensable. Did changing patterns and habits in your life mean that you became unrecognizable and forgotten? Could you ever find yourself again if you needed to come back? Would anybody write?

I had no Scandinavian ancestors, no rosemalled wooden chest in the attic that had survived customs at Ellis Island. Not having a Swedish heritage suddenly seemed like a deficit. If I'd had a grandmother who knew how to bake *tunnbröd,* eat herring, and knock back aquavit at midsummer, I might have felt I was returning to home waters. But I exist because of various intimacies between people from Ireland, Scotland, England, and Alsace-Lorraine. I am a true American mongrel.

My great-great-grandparents had left their lives in Europe a century earlier for new lives in a new land. Didn't their reasons for leaving mean anything to me?

Late that spring Lars returned to Gimdalen to prepare for the fishing season on Idsjöströmmen. I remained in Bozeman until Peter finished the school year. Having moved out of his former residence, part of Lars's preparations included finding us a house to rent. This was not going to be an easy task, since almost every house in the village that was habitable was occupied. The day after he arrived, however, he called to announce success.

"I've found a house for us to live in. It's the Rislund house, the only one available. It's rather small, but the price is good. We only have to pay for the electricity we use."

He was almost out of breath with excitement.

"It's the old Rislund house, where Edith Winnberg's mother and uncles used to live. Edith rents to fishermen during the summer and to the Sami when they graze their reindeer near the village during the winter. There's only a slight problem. It doesn't have a bathroom. It has an outhouse."

I was silent.

"All the summer cottages have an outhouse. It's very clean and nice. Everyone is going to the outhouse. You'll see. You'll like it."

"It will be like camping," I offered finally, trying to sound positive.

"Yes, something like that."

I wondered if there was plumbing. "Is there water?"

"Only in the kitchen. We can rent a shower from our neighbors. I talked to them yesterday and they said they wouldn't mind if we used their bathroom to take showers.

We can pay them. Or we can bathe in the lake. Everything will be fine. We'll be together. Don't worry."

"Okay."

My son, who had grown into a six-year-old boy with curly brown hair, his dark-brown eyes framed by round wire-rimmed glasses, easily caught on to my enthusiasm for our new life and the promise of adventure. He seemed completely at ease with the idea of traveling to Sweden. Until the night before we were to leave. After I had tucked him into bed he announced, "Mom, I can't go to Sweden."

"Why?" I asked, alarmed.

"Because there are trolls there."

I wasn't really clear about troll life in Sweden, but I realized I had better come up with something quick. "There aren't any trolls there. Trolls are not real," I explained.

"How do you know?"

"They only exist in folktales."

"What if you're wrong?"

"If I am wrong, then ... well ... they're very small, like ants. If you come across one all you have to do is step on it."

Later that night I checked to see if Peter had finally fallen asleep. The comforter rose and fell with his rhythmic breathing. Silently I thanked him for following me with such blind trust, for letting me haul him halfway around the globe to live with a man in a house without hot running water in the middle of a forest full of trolls. Quietly I pulled the door shut.

Long after midnight, when lists had been checked for the fiftieth time and the message on the answering machine had been changed from "You have reached ..." to "We're not at home right now ...," I finally finished packing fishing gear, waders, wading boots, fly rods, camera equipment, books, shoes, and clothes. I parked three bags next to the door, to wait like well-trained dogs until morning light.

Early the next day, my drowsy child and I walked out the door, leaving behind the sounds of western rivers swelling with spring runoff, the sweet smells of cottonwoods exuding their pungent scent into sun-warmed air, the red-winged blackbirds calling for their mates. It would be the first time in nearly twenty summers that I could not look forward to a walk along a Montana stream, where I might see the surface dimple from a rainbow trout sipping down a dun, then, warned by the vibrations of my step, see the fish flee to deeper water. I would miss the frisking newborn bison and the cut-throat trout in Yellowstone Park; the Fourth of July, the chance to spot a bear, and the great expanse of sky that makes you feel your vision is sharp and in focus every day. No Rocky Mountains to turn pink in the melancholy light of dusk. I would miss the smell of rain that came before I could feel it, the rumble of afternoon thunderstorms, and the flashes of lightning that made me flinch and, with shoulders hunched, offer up prayers to spare my life.

I would not see drift boats slipping by on their way down the Madison River, announced only by hushed voices of fishermen and squeaks from the oarlocks. I would not see the grasshoppers of August that could be trapped with a cupped hand, crippled with a pinch, and tossed into the river for a trout to take. I would not feel the ninety-degree days cooled by the forty-degree nights. I sighed. Time to go.

Our plane taxied east, toward the sun rising above the Bridger Mountains, and began rocketing down the runway. Holding my son's hand and looking out the window, I

watched the landscape that for many years had been my refuge and safe harbor blur with the speed of our leaving. The
roar of the engines vibrated in my chest as, open throttle, we
were pushed toward a new summer, another country, another
river, another life, and, with wheels up, a wind, like faith,
lifted our metallic wings and carried us away.

Arrival

THE 747'S DESCENT was as familiar to me as walking down stairs. Flight attendants pushed through the cabin, offering the last of the air service—scalding-hot towels to freshen up faces and necks. Peter pushed my hand away as I nudged and jostled him.

"Peter, we're here. We're landing in Sweden. Wake up."

Beneath us the familiar red-and-white farmhouses came into view. These buildings, their boxed shapes and angled roofs designed to slip snow during the long winters, repeat

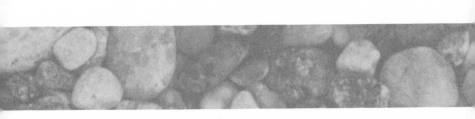

themselves like a refrain from the coastlines to the mountains. They may differ here and there—a porch here or a balcony there—but they are all hard-won islands of farmland within a vast green sea of trees, stretching from horizon to horizon; the houses looked as practical and determined as the people who built them.

Lakes shimmered in the morning light—so many they couldn't possibly all have names—and as the plane continued to gently descend all we could see were a mass of conifers, making it look as if we were about to land on a Christmas tree farm.

It was eight-thirty in the morning, local Stockholm time. Thick with sleepiness and in need of a toothbrush we shuffled off the plane into the terminal. Bright-eyed Scandinavian and European businessmen and -women stepped briskly past us, leaving behind scented trails of boutique colognes. I piled our baggage, and Peter, onto a cart, and steered toward the domestic terminal to catch the fifty-minute flight to Östersund, where Lars waited for us.

The last flight took us to the heart of the Swedish countryside. The people with us on this part of the flight were almost all Swedes, making me feel we had made our final transition to this other world. The chill in the air when we landed reminded me that Sweden is a place for people who don't mind the sting of fresh wind or coolness in their summer nights. In this country, you need sturdy shoes to walk on gravel and dirt roads or ancient cobbled streets. You need a jacket in the early part of the summer and a bathing suit in August. Sweden is a country about nature and being in it.

Lars, the only man holding a dozen red roses, encircled us

both in his arms. The long, tiring journey slipped off my shoulders as I felt his embrace.

Cool air blew through the rolled-down window as we drove toward Gimdalen. The radio played Elvis singing "All Shook Up," then ABBA—that legendary Swedish pop-rock group—harmonized a snappy tune called "Take a Chance on Me." The song after that was a folk song played on a violin. Clouds gathered above us, but when it could, the sun radiated strong warm rays over the green and lush countryside.

Just over an hour later, we turned onto the gravel road that followed the eastern edge of Idsjön. Whitecaps rocked across the surface and slapped into the shoreline. Soon we topped the hill at the north entrance to Gimdalen, and the entire neighborhood of red-and-white houses and farm buildings appeared. It was the clean, quiet, and shy place with the strong, trustworthy square houses and farm buildings that I remembered. In one of the larger courtyards, a white flagpole, at least five stories high, carried the Swedish colors: a sun-yellow cross on a sky-blue background. Swedish flags are flown for major holidays, birthdays, graduations, confirmations, and any other occasion that seems fitting. After all the planning and worrying about how to manage a cross-Atlantic lifestyle, Lars and I had finally taken the first major step. For me it felt like a day a flag should be flown.

Lars turned off the main road and onto a narrow lane. A woman was preparing the soil for a garden near her house. She did not look up as we drove past. That didn't mean she had not seen us, nor did it mean she didn't already know I was American and had a young son. In time I would learn that the village knows all. Not that the Gimdaleners mean to be nosy, but news is news and it travels. They knew which house Lars and I were staying in (and who had lived and died there), and that it was old and had no shower, which surely prompted a discussion and a few chuckles as they summed up our situation saying, *It must be love!* And of course they knew Lars, for he had married a woman from the village and they had raised their twin boys here.

In Bozeman, a city of over forty thousand, I felt anonymous and left it up to the local paper to give me information about what was going on in the community. But in Gimdalen I would learn the art of observation. I would learn how to tune in to the sight of a passing car, or smoke rising from a chimney, and realize I had just gathered information that might come in handy later on if someone should ask, "Have you seen Claus?" and I could answer, "Yes, he left around four o'clock. He also left his woodstove burning."

In a place where it is public knowledge who is going to paint what house even before scaffolding goes up, it is sporting to stay on top of things. Trading information is a little like trading baseball cards: *If you tell me what happened to Mikael after the barn dance, I'll tell you who she was.* The number of cars parked in front of the Månssons' tells everyone that there are visitors from Stockholm. The light in Bengt Persson's living room late in the evening means he is watching TV or tying flies. This harmless but useful information represents the collective routine of life in the village. Irregularities are obvious. Bank robbers beware: you might hide from the world in a small village but not for long. Give the villagers five minutes and they'll know what time you arrived, the color and make of your car, where you're from, and how many times you've been married.

At the same time, however, being labeled a gossip is not desirable. To avoid this, you do your best to appear uninterested in the woman seen lately at Roland's house, or in the new boat on the lake—even if you are just dying to know. You share what you know carefully. Experience teaches that what goes around comes around.

Twenty-four hours after leaving Montana, we arrived at long last at the house Lars had so enthusiastically talked about on the phone weeks earlier. It looked the way I felt—exhausted. Built in the early twenties, it had apparently been painted only twice since then, and whatever color it had been was faded to a grayish green and was flaking. The landlord had placed a potted red geranium on the inside sill behind a cracked front window.

Lars unbuckled his seat belt, called to Peter to wake up, and prepared to get out of the car. I grabbed his shirtsleeve.

"Is this it?"

Lars looked in the direction of my pointing finger.

"Yes."

I smiled halfheartedly.

We climbed a set of rusted iron steps that might once have been painted green and unlocked the front door. The entry hall was dark. I half expected to hear someone playing a saw. The door to the right led to the kitchen. Lars pulled it open.

"In the country, this is where everyone gathers," he said with the authority of a tour guide.

"Cue bats," I mumbled to myself.

The green wallpaper had plate-sized daisies that looked like man-eaters. I imagined skeletal remains in the avocado-green cabinets. A rickety table and three mismatched sky-blue wooden chairs stood beneath a generous-sized window.

Despite the darkening sky outside, light managed to reach the room.

A traditional benchlike couch, the same blue color as the chairs, was positioned under a second window. Lars explained that since people treat the kitchen like a living room, almost every Swedish kitchen has a sofa. Some, like ours, are used as a couch by day and a bed by night. To turn the couch into a bed, the seat covering is removed revealing the empty boxed area beneath the seat. Then the front part of the couch slides out like a drawer widening it enough so two people can sleep there. Pillows and blankets can make it quite cozy, Lars assured us. Its high sides protect occupants from drafts, yet allow them to be warmed by the kitchen fire. Some Swedish sofas are quite elaborate, with carved backs and scrolled arms. The one in our kitchen was plain. It reminded me of a coffin.

From the kitchen we walked through to the family room, where Lars had made up a little cot for Peter. It had two pillows and a gold-colored bedspread neatly tucked into place. The room had gold-flocked wallpaper with vertical stripes, a TV with foil wrapped around the antennae, bookshelves crowded with Lars's collection of fishing books, including signed copies of *Keeper of the Stream* and *Nymphs and the Trout* by Frank Sawyer.

The next doorway led to the room that would serve as both our bedroom and office. It had fancy green-flocked wallpaper, a ginger-colored bureau for our clothes, yet more bookshelves, Lars's writing desk, and a phone. Hanging crookedly from the ceiling was a light fixture with six bulbs at the end of curled brass arms, each capped by a dusty little shade. The mattresses we would sleep on were tidily made up and lying side by side on the floor. No curtains were on the windows.

From this room a door opened out into the entry hall. You could run in a circle through the entire downstairs by going from the entry hall to the kitchen, to Peter's room, to our room, and back out to the entry hall—which, I suspected, is exactly what you might feel like doing on some long winter days.

Off the hall were stairs leading to an unfinished second story. In the early part of the century, Lars explained, it was customary to finish the first floor with the understanding that in time money would become available to finish the second floor (much like the American habit of planning to finish a basement later). Curtains were often hung in the windows to create the illusion from the outside that it was in use. But somehow money was never allocated to finish the second floor and it became a storage space (much like those unfinished American basements).

Braving the darkness and loose stair boards, I crept up to have a look. The second story was as big as the first, but it lacked walls and insulation. Two-by-four joists had been installed, and dried moss and sawdust spread as insulation, but there were no floorboards. I balanced on top of the joists and stepped into the room. Clothing that had once belonged to Edith's mother and uncles hung on a clothesline tied between exposed posts and lay on top of old tables like offerings at a yard sale. There were men's plaid flannel shirts and thin cotton boxer shorts. On a bureau was a shaving kit with a boar-hair brush and a package of rusted single-edged blades. A pair of dark wool pants that looked as if they had fit a short, thick-waisted man were draped over the door to a freestanding closet. Protruding from the bottom of the closet were a pair of women's sturdy black shoes with square practical heels, the kind old women wore to church decades ago. I picked them up. The owner had had small feet, maybe a size 6. I looked into the closet, where a dark navy-blue dress with white polka dots hung like a scarecrow. I quickly put the shoes down, hoping not to have offended her ghost.

Trunks with tarnished metal bindings and latches, sagging shelves, and stacks of old papers and magazines crowded the room. It was apparent that this was a place where mosquitoes and wasps sought refuge from the heat during the summer, and snow drifted in during the winter. Spiderwebs hung on the inside corners of windows, which, I found, would open, letting the smell of the impending rain rush in.

The whole house suffered from age and a lack of imagination and cash flow. It told a story about lives that had gotten stuck. The people who had called the place home had gone as far as they could before time had caught up with them, and then, as if they'd been popped right out of their shoes, they disappeared.

I jumped, startled, as the galvanized metal roof loudly snapped in response to a drop in temperature outside. I heard Lars wadding up newspaper in the kitchen below to start a fire in the woodstove. Peter, breathless with excitement, met me at the bottom of the stairs.

"Mom, you gotta see the outhouse! It's cool!"

The outhouse was an extension of the woodshed. A birch tree near the door shielded it from the neighbors who lived directly behind us; otherwise they would have had even more to talk about with the other villagers. Lars had spruced it up, swept the floor, brought in a carpet, and put up posters. One poster had a drawing of a woman sitting on a three-legged stool, milking a cow in a meadow near a lake. Another illustrated Birds of the Forest. Another advertised a fly-fishing exposition in Holland. The last poster, put out by the local tourist bureau, had a photo of Lars fishing. An ample supply of magazines in both English and Swedish graced the bench where two symmetrical holes with matching lids had been cut.

"Why are there two places to go?" asked Peter.

Maybe it meant you could bring a friend, or you had your own—like your personalized coffee cup at work.

"That way no one has to wait in line," I replied.

Next I did what you know you shouldn't do. I lifted one of the lids and looked down. I couldn't help it. Waste from the people who had lived there before was piled up like petrified wood.

"Eeeeww! Is that poop?" exclaimed my observant six-year-old. Shooing Peter out the door, I quickly latched it behind us.

Smoke from Lars's fire drifted up from the chimney, making it seem more like the beginning of fall than the beginning of summer. Peter went to his new room to get a book. I settled myself on the kitchen sofa and watched Lars prepare dinner over the woodstove. Rain began to fall outside. Lars was so happy to finally have us with him. In celebration he presented me with a glass of Chardonnay.

"To the summer, to the river, and to us," he toasted.

That was when the monstrous green wallpaper, the red houses, and all those trees started to swim in front of me. I couldn't remember who he was or why I had come. Suddenly I was very afraid of him and what passion had made me do. I worried that I might end up like those poor people whose clothes had been left behind to rot. I wanted to slap us both awake. Tears welled up and a great sob broke loose from my chest. Lars took my glass, put it on the kitchen counter next to his, went down on his knees, took me by the shoulders, looked into my eyes, and tenderly asked me what was the matter.

I couldn't tell him that I didn't know what I had been thinking when I had agreed to come to Sweden, or that Peter and I might not last a week. Instead I said, "I missed you." He lifted his eyebrows sympathetically and put his arms around me.

"I missed you, and I'm really tired," I said.

He hugged me tight. My tears soaked into his shirt.

The River

EARLY THE NEXT MORNING the two new American residents of the Rislund rental shuffled to the kitchen in stocking feet and shivered while Lars energetically stoked the wood-burning stove and made tea. Summer comes slowly above the sixty degree north latitude. May mornings begin with a temperature near forty degrees. Summer temperatures remain cool through June and July, ranging between fifty-five and sixty-five degrees. The highs in August average near seventy. Starting the day huddled next to the woodstove would continue through mid-July. We held our tea mugs with both hands.

My eyes were puffy from tears and a night of heavy sleep. I sat in a mini-stupor, once again contemplating my surroundings. Lars had laid the table with a blue-and-white–checked cloth and put out a variety of breads, cheeses, and jams, a basket of *knäckebröd* (rye crisp bread) broken into pieces, and a bowl of hard-boiled eggs. He had even thought to give Peter his own special mug; it had a teddy bear painted on the side. While I sliced a piece of Jarlsberg cheese and placed it on a piece of *knäckebröd,* Lars brought what looked like a tube of toothpaste to the table.

"Here, Peter, try some Kalle's Caviar on your egg. Magnus and Fredrik loved this at your age," said Lars, squeezing a khaki-colored mass of fish eggs out of the tube onto my son's hard-boiled egg.

Peter is not as squeamish about food as I am. Lars had already successfully introduced him to Stilton, Gorgonzola, and Camembert. On weekends after dinner, Lars and Peter would sit together at the head of the table and eat slices of these cheeses the way some people eat birthday cake. I had always remained at a safe distance.

Kalle's Caviar was a hit. Peter greedily squeezed a dab and a squiggle on every bite of egg he popped in his mouth. I had tried the stuff the last time I was in Sweden and found it too strong for my white-bread taste buds.

After watching Peter happily interact with his food, and having my teacup filled for the second time, I realized how many continuous and thoughtful efforts were being made to help a boy and his mother feel at home. Maybe I could ignore the wallpaper. The outhouse wasn't that bad; I'd get used to the circle of chill on my butt each time I sat down. As for the upstairs, we could move the old clothing off to the side and use the clothesline for our own shirts and pants.

I reached for Lars's hand and squeezed it. He smiled with relief to see me looking more at ease. Around the table we quietly sipped our tea, while the kitchen warmed and the clouds started to part, allowing a corner of blue sky to shine through.

Besides finding us a house to rent, Lars had purchased a secondhand car at the gas station in Bräcke. It was a faded yellow 1979 Mercedes sedan that had just arrived and was going for the bargain price of nineteen hundred dollars. The car had a little rust around the wheel wells and made strange squealing sounds when you started it up. It also made puttering sounds when you drove it, and sputtering sounds when you stopped. There was no power steering and it took leaded gas. But Lars was happy to have found anything on such short notice.

The first order of business was to see the river. After breakfast we dressed warmly, wearing long johns under our jeans, and headed out. Squealing and puttering, the car got us to the main road and through the village. I saw a curtain being gently pulled aside, doubtless to give someone a better view of Lars and his new family. A woman out walking her dog looked up and smiled as we drove by. At the southern entrance to the village, the road winds gently downhill through dense forest right to Idsjöströmmen.

We stood on the bridge that spans the river and listened as water washed noisily beneath us. The bridge is simple: one lane wide, twenty feet over the water's surface, a city block long, and made of steel and concrete. It was designed to support fully loaded logging trucks. It is also the physical boundary marking the beginning of Lars's leased section. We leaned over the railing, my hand firmly grasping the back of Peter's pants, and looked for grayling, which should have made their annual migration into the river to spawn a month before.

The river, containing the remains of winter, spilled high and clear from Idsjön, tumbling heedlessly around and over protruding boulders like stampeding cattle. Runoff here is not the cloudy mud bath it is in Montana. Melting snows in the Rockies and Yellowstone Park pull soil from clear cuts and overgrazed fields and slide into tributary creeks that in turn flow into the main rivers, resulting in earth-colored waters that remain unfishable until the runoff passes through. It usually takes most of May and part of June before the Gallatin River can be fished, and the Yellowstone River can be unfishable until mid-July.

Idsjöströmmen has a light amber color, like the underbelly of a brown trout, and chartreuse patches of aquatic moss grow on top of some of the submerged rocks. Its waters are clear even during runoff, since any soil carried into the river system from the Scandinavian mountain range, hundreds of miles to the west, settles in the numerous lakes that link river to river like a string of pearls.

Idsjöströmmen's pools remain deep and dark. No sunlight illuminates their greatest depths, but when the sun blinked through the clouds we scanned the runs and riffled waters where grayling hold and feed, looking for their shadows undulating in the currents. Waves, ripples, and glare made it difficult to see. Wearing polarized glasses, we stared hard, seeking the irregular flat spot on the surface that, like a windowpane, would offer a brief view. Light suddenly revealed the secrets of the river: fish trying to live anonymous lives.

"There!" I shouted, pointing off to my right.

"Yes. See, there are two," said Lars.

"More over here," I announced, pointing directly below.

"They are everywhere!" said Lars with delight.

The grayling were in. Seeing them encouraged us. Opening day, June first, was only a week away. There would be fish to fish for.

————

LARS RESERVED OPENING DAY just for us. We wanted to be the first to check the fishing conditions, so that we would have something to report to the fly fishers scheduled to arrive the next morning. We suited up in waders, wading boots, and fishing vests. Lars also carried a backpack with lunch, eating utensils, plates, rain jackets, and extra clothes (in case someone fell in, which often happens on the first day of fishing after a long winter), as well as an ax for chopping wood. Peter joined us, outfitted in knee-high rubber boots and, should his curiosity land him in the water, a bright orange life jacket. Lars whittled the twigs and leaves off a fallen branch and handed it to Peter, who marched happily ahead of us, stabbing his new walking stick into the soft ground as he went. We walked downstream under the canopy of forest until we reached the second windbreak, where we stashed the gear and the lunch we had brought.

Before fishing, we gathered wood for what I thought was going to be the lunchtime fire. Lars returned from his search with fairly large pieces of birch, placed them near a tree stump, and removed the long-handled ax from the backpack. The heavy steel head of the ax hit the birch with decisive force. *CHOP*. Wood chips flew. Again, *CHOP*. The birch branch was transformed into kindling. Peter looked on in admiration. Lars quietly told him how to stand with legs apart and how to keep his fingers away from the blade; then he handed Peter the ax. I calculated that, driving at top speed, it would take forty-five minutes to get to the nearest emergency room, and began to protest.

Two sullen-faced males turned to look at me.

"I will take care of Peter," said Lars, dismissing me with a wave of his hand. "Go fishing."

Peter's face brightened.

Slowly backing up, I watched the two of them standing by the chopping block. Peter took a swing with the ax. I winced as the wood split with a crack. Lars praised Peter for a job well done. Next he demonstrated how to start the fire with the birch's papery bark, then after adding bigger pieces, we watched it grow. The idea was that chopping wood and feeding the fire would keep Peter entertained while Lars and I fished nearby. I wasn't sure how Child Protective Services would view the parenting skills of a mother who left her six-year-old behind to play with an ax and fire while she went out fishing, but reluctantly I turned away from the growing flames and stepped into the river. I heard behind me: *CHOP. CHOP. CHOP*. With each strike of the ax I imagined a severed finger or a splintered shin. I struggled with the impulse to go back and stand over him.

I thought back to Peter's birth, to that moment when he made the transition between life as a fish to life as a human. I had held my breath during those moments of terrible silence as my pewter-colored baby was lifted away from my body and encouraged to breathe. I had watched the doctor suction my son's nose and mouth until, after what seemed to be an eternity, the long, regular wail of a baby finally filled the room.

"He's all right," said the doctor.

This combination of noise and children being a good thing was one of the first lessons I learned as a mother. As long as I could hear Peter chopping, perhaps—perhaps—I could believe he was all right. Oddly enough, the smell of wood smoke and the sound of chopping soon became a comfort, easing my maternal angst. I faced the river and began to fish.

Now in its fifth year as a managed fishery, Idsjöströmmen was showing signs of recovery. Biologists from the University of Umeå, headed by a man named Ingemar Näslund, had studied the effects of catch-and-release on wild grayling. No other river in Sweden (or in Scandinavia, for that matter) afforded this opportunity, because no other river had ever been so carefully managed. After taking visual counts by floating the river in dry suits, compiling catch reports, and tagging and measuring fish, the biologists had discovered that the size and numbers of grayling were climbing. The first year under Lars's care, the average grayling caught was eleven inches in length. Three years later, the average size was sixteen inches. The fish were thriving. A river was healing. Its reputation among fly fishers was growing as well, with the number of booked fishing days rising each year. This was the result Lars had hoped for.

Even so, the improvements that fly fishers and biologists saw in Idsjöströmmen were not universally appreciated. Some people did not like the new restrictions and rules, particularly not the idea of returning fish after playing them. One well-known fishing artist and author who summered in the village let it be known that he was against Lars's conservation practices and claimed that the new restrictions and fees excluded the average fisher; only the wealthy would have an opportunity to fish. He took his protests to newspapers and magazines. The controversy grew into a heated debate within the Swedish fishing community. People who had once fished the river boycotted it. A Scandinavian fly-fishing magazine that had formerly published articles by and about Lars blacklisted him. It also refused to print any articles about Idsjöströmmen. Some former fishing partners stopped calling. The question was, how could a Swede who had grown up under *Allemansrätten* think of regulating a fishery?

Allemansrätten, meaning roughly "right of public access," has been deeply embedded in Swedish life for hundreds of years. It allows everyone access to the Swedish countryside, regardless of boundaries. Everyone has the right to roam freely in the woods, fields, or on the beaches. People may walk across private land, pick and/or sell the berries and mushrooms they find there, camp, make fires, ride horses, and boat or swim anywhere, so long as they keep a respectful distance from dwellings. No barbed wire, no hunter-orange–marked posts declaring NO TRESPASSING, no complicated gate latches or bullet-hole–riddled boundary markers, such as are found in Montana. I could understand how people used to unlimited access to nature might be upset by the new rules that governed Idsjöströmmen. In addition, in Sweden, as a Social Democratic society, there is a pervasive feeling that everything should be available to everybody. Limiting access to fishing appeared to be not only a direct attack on the locals' established ways of doing things, but on Swedish culture itself.

My thoughts were interrupted by the sight of a purple-red dorsal fin: a grayling had just snatched my fly. Grayling were certainly not the trout I had grown up with. Unlike rainbow or brown trout, they did not bring back treasured memories of walks along the banks of the Madison River through spicy sagebrush with a pocket full of Royal Wulffs. They were never mentioned in the conversations I heard in fly shops (though I did hear they were delicious when cooked streamside in Alaska), nor were they part of my earliest dreams about casting and catching. I had assumed my life was going to be defined by trout. I did not know that one day I would start a new life with a grayish fish with a forked tail, or that this aquatic-insect–eating, dry-fly–biting creature would swim its way into my fly-fishing heart. Call me sentimental, but there is something endearing about a fish that drapes its dorsal fin over the female to hold her close during spawning.

Grayling on Idsjöströmmen require accurate presentations with fine tippet, drag-free drifts, and persistence on the part of the angler. They take in their own good time, and when they do, they approach the fly with very untroutlike behavior. A trout will opportunistically wait for food to come by. A grayling, on the other hand, will rush from depths of six feet or more, a mini-torpedo fired from the river bottom, to take a dry fly off the surface. Sometimes when you set the hook, grayling will leap before it, tearing back to the dark waters of the river, bucking and jerking all the way.

The grayling I had on the line was feisty with fight. I played it until it tired. In one swift movement I raised the rod tip and netted my fish. The barbless fly I had caught it with loosened and dropped out of the grayling's mouth. With both hands I reached in and lifted the fish up out of the net. "You're all right," I said to the grayling. Gently I lowered it beneath quiet water near the bank, loosely cradling its belly in my hands. I watched and waited. The grayling's gills pumped in rhythmic beats while it caught its liquid breath. The instant the grayling recovered, it wriggled its tail and returned home.

CHOP. CHOP. CHOP.

I glanced backward toward the bank and saw a very contented child supplying his new best friend—the fire—with wood. What if I had been too afraid to let him try? What if I had stayed on the other side of the world among the familiar sagebrush and trout? What if the fishing board hadn't given Lars a chance to manage the river? Blowing up the river for logs, restoring it. Killing all the fish, putting them back. Living in one country, then another. First trout, then grayling. Breathing in, breathing out. *CHOP. CHOP. You're all right.*

Wading with Staffan

EIGHT BUSINESSMEN from the nearby city of Östersund arrived one morning at Idsjöströmmen's first windbreak and inaugurated their fly-fishing weekend with a toast. Small hand-crafted birch cups with carved reindeer bone handles, each carrying a throat full of Bushmans Finest, had been ceremoniously handed to us by quiet, middle-aged Sven, their host. Bearded like a sea captain, wearing a brown, weatherworn fishing hat, a blue plaid flannel shirt, and dark-green cargo pants, Sven praised the river and the day ahead before saluting the group with a nod and a raised cup. They downed his whiskey in one smooth toss, nodded politely to each other, then gazed toward the fire, which would remain lit the entire time they were on the river.

While I waited for a sign that we should begin fishing, I looked over and read the whiskey bottle's label. In English it said:

> *Made specially for the tough people who find their pleasure in the woods and sometimes in the bottle. It'll make you beautiful and it'll make you smell like a real man from the good old days.*

I looked into my cup and smiled. Sven thought I wanted more and reached to serve me. Being beautiful was one thing, but smelling "like a real man from the good old days" was another. I didn't want to chance it. I shook my head and stepped back.

Lars and I had been hired to guide these gentlemen. They wanted us to suggest places for them to fish and to help those who required it. We were invited to join them for lunch, which they had organized and would prepare. This is not how things go in the States, or at least not in Montana. There, fly-fishing guides are expected to bring and serve the lunch. More important, like a good hunting dog, they are not to leave their client's side except to go to the bathroom. American guides must have an engaging personality. A cache of jokes is helpful. They are expected to know where the fish are and to make them bite. If the fish aren't biting they must change the client's flies until they do. If the client is inept and loses his temper, the guide must have a knack for telling the client what he's doing wrong without upsetting him further.

The client should be guided into landing the largest fish of the season, preferably before cocktail hour.

A Swedish fly fisher, by contrast, takes more responsibility for his own fishing. He becomes even quieter than usual if a guide not only stands next to him while he fishes, but starts to tell him how he should be fishing and what he should be fishing with. A Swedish fly fisher doesn't mind attending a fishing seminar or being given instruction in a classroom as long as he can return to the water and practice in private. But he'd rather you drank the last of his Absolut and stole all the tires off his Volvo than actually guide him.

"Jennifer, you will work with Staffan and Mikael."

Staffan and Mikael were the beginners in the group. They nodded and headed off to collect their rods. Two others followed Lars for a casting lesson. The rest held a brief discussion about what section of the river they wanted to fish and, as important, when to meet for lunch. Then, like a hatch in a high wind, we all scattered to various locations up and down Idsjöströmmen.

My charges stood respectfully in front of me. Mikael was in his late twenties, and though he had been labeled a beginner, he had rigged his fly rod by himself.

"Have you fly fished before?" I asked.

Both Mikael and Staffan nodded.

"Would you like me to show you where to fish?"

They both nodded again. Mikael stepped forward, eager to be on his way.

"Mikael, you fish this area here. What fly do you have on? You know how to fish dry fly? Yes? You fish that rock, all the way down," I said, pointing at the river with the tip of my rod and making a waving motion with my hand. "Lots of fish there."

Mikael smiled, stepped down the side of the bank, and entered the river.

I turned my attention to Staffan. Staffan was in his late fifties, slender, and had a kind face. I think he felt sorry for me. He would have been content to go off and discover the fishing on his own, but he seemed to understand that I needed something to do.

"How is your English?" I asked him.

"I understand more than I speak," Staffan answered.

"The same with me and Swedish," I explained. "We can speak part English-Swedish. Our own language, no?"

Staffan smiled.

Because it was near the end of spring runoff, the river was going to be tough to wade. A wading staff is a necessity on Idsjöströmmen at any time of the year, but more so when the river is up. The water rolled and rushed past, warning me to wade carefully into fishable runs and pools.

The place I wanted to reach was about fifty feet into the current. I planned our traverse so that the deepest the water would get would be about midthigh. After negotiating our way around a few boulders, digging in with our heels, and wedging our staffs between the rocks, we would end up standing calf-deep, secure in our position at the top of a deep, grayling-filled pool. First, however, the leader and line had to be made ready.

My recommendation for the fishing was a prince nymph, weighted a foot above the fly with a bead of soft lead called a split shot to help it sink. At the river's edge, I asked for Staffan's rod, then inspected and prepared his leader. I cut off his old fly and handed it back to him. I quickly tied on the prince nymph, took out the split shot, and squeezed it onto the leader with my fishing pliers. I planned to use the weight of this rig not only to get the fly down quickly in the fast-moving current, but to make casting easier for Staffan, since it was his first attempt at fly fishing on a river (he was already an accomplished spin caster). All he would need to do was take one well-executed back cast, push forward to land the leader and fly, and let the line swing downstream in front of us.

I felt Staffan's intent gaze. I had taken his rod. I had taken his leader. I glanced up at his face as I tied on a tippet, wondering if he might be having an anxiety attack due to a combination of not being able to voice any objections in English, not wanting to offend, wondering what people would think if they saw him being waited on, and, to top it off, having to internalize all these emotions. All this left him staring helplessly but with intense interest at what I was doing with his gear.

Finally I finished rigging his rod and cheerfully announced that we were ready. I hooked the fly on the third guide from the rod tip, looped the leader around the reel, and tightened everything so that nothing would come loose while we waded. Staffan received his rod in silence.

Wading staff in hand, I again gauged the force of the current. Staffan and I began by stepping into a slow, shallow area. I knew that soon we would feel the power of the river pick up, and that it would be a dicey shuffle to our casting position. I did what any conscientious guide would do back in the States: I extended my right arm for Staffan to hold and steady himself.

To brace himself against the rush of water, which was growing stronger with each step, Staffan would need to grasp my forearm near my elbow and I his. This way, we would be able to support each other without losing our balance. I waved for him to come closer. I tapped the underside of my forearm, and demonstrated what I wanted him to do. Staffan did what only a self-respecting Swede could do. He shook his head. I tapped my forearm again, thinking he might have misunderstood. He smiled and shook his head, then took a step back. I looked at the way the river churned past us. I looked at Staffan, who had seemed less frail earlier. I looked downstream and wondered where he might land after the current had swept him off his feet. Staffan waited and leaned on his staff while I paused. He wasn't going to give me his arm.

I looked upstream. Mikael had found his way to a rock that rose above the current, and was contentedly flinging his line into the run I had pointed out to him. Another fly fisher opposite Mikael was casting to the inside edge of what looked like a promising riffle. Though I wanted to be farther out in the current, if I held back and kept Staffan in calmer water, I wouldn't have to worry about him falling in. But the grayling were not in the quiet water. The one clear thing was that he wasn't going to give me his arm.

Waiting for my next instruction, Staffan stood upright and proud. He knew nothing about my internal debate. He had never fly fished or waded in a river like this before. He was a man who had gotten this far in life without needing anyone to steady him, yet he was my responsibility. I squinted, and looked across the river, then downstream.

My American clients would have let me carry them into

the river on my back if they thought it would get them a fish. I recalled the last day I worked as a guide for a couple from California. We had fished Depuy's Spring Creek just outside Livingston, Montana, and from early morning to late afternoon the man had insisted on flipping his line and fly at me whenever a piece of grass or vegetation got stuck on the hook. "Could you help me with that?" he had asked. Each time I obligingly took the fly in hand and removed the grass.

Suddenly it became clear what I needed to do.

"Staffan!" I said, loudly enough so that he could hear me above the roar of the river. He looked sharply in my direction. I pointed first at him, then at myself, then at my arm, and made that request all travelers should know how to make in the language of the country they are visiting—*hjälp mig* (help me). With a bright smile, Staffan sprang forward and reached for my arm.

For the last twenty-five feet of our crossing, we clutched our wading staffs, which we stabbed down into the river bed. Forearms locked in a firm embrace, we moved together against the current. Finally we reached our goal, and Staffan was able to stand without support. He made clean, tangle-free casts, and the pool gave us two beautiful grayling before lunch.

Visitors

"OSKAR DIED in that sofa."

Our neighbor Carl-Åke pointed at the kitchen sofa I was sitting on, the one that pulled out into a bed. His mother and grandmother had lived in the house we were renting, and Oskar was an aged uncle who had lived there with them. Carl-Åke stirred sugar into his coffee, tapped his spoon against the rim of his cup, and rested it on the saucer.

"My great-grandmother lived here too. But she died before Oskar. She was very old."

Carl-Åke sipped his coffee.

"My grandmother, she was a baker. She baked cakes. Wedding cakes. A very cheerful woman. She died here two years ago. She wasn't sick or anything like that. She just went to sleep. My wife and I found her the next day, not in the sofa, but in the room where you and Lars-Åke sleep."

Carl-Åke took another sip of coffee.

"How do you like Sweden?"

———

IN THE SWEDISH COUNTRYSIDE, visitors knock on the door before entering. Should the door be unlocked, they do not have to wait for you to answer; they step inside, take off their shoes, and in stocking feet find their way into the kitchen, where someone is usually cooking, eating, or conversing. Visitors stopping by at dinnertime do not need to leave and come back later. They sit on the kitchen sofa and talk to you while you eat.

One of our regular visitors was Bengt, a bachelor. Actually, he is divorced and has two children, but I never knew him when he was married, and he always seemed lonely, so I always thought of him as a bachelor. Bengt's family has had a presence in Gimdalen for over a hundred years. His mother and all three of his brothers and their families live in the village, and have since the day they were born. His innumerable cousins, aunts, uncles, nephews, and nieces live there too. It is not unusual in villages like this that nearly everyone is related to nearly everyone else. Bengt has known Lars for many years, and though Bengt didn't fish Idsjöströmmen, he was interested in the river and stopped by once a week to get the latest reports.

Sometimes, when Bengt and Lars were talking, the phone

rang and Lars went to answer it, leaving Bengt and me alone. Bengt spoke English rather well, but when we were left alone he often lapsed into long stretches of painful silence. When the silence lasted to the point where I felt like running out of the room, he would say, "*Ja-ha . . . ,*" the Swedish equivalent of "Yep, so . . . ," and then, with a hand on each knee, turn his face upward and stare at the ceiling.

Once, when Lars was on the phone and Bengt was studying the ceiling, he suddenly looked at me and blurted, "In the Mediterranean, people are dying of sunstroke."

Stunned, I nodded in acknowledgment of this news flash. He added quickly, "More rain tomorrow. No mosquitoes."

Our heads nodded in sync until silence embraced us once more.

Sometimes Bengt would stop looking at the ceiling, fold his arms across his chest, and mutter *mmm,* in a tone that suggested he was agreeing with me, even though we hadn't been discussing anything. A few seconds would pass, then he would go *mmm* again. *Mmm* also seemed to be a sort of compliment, as in, "*Mmm*—everything is fine," or "*Mmm*—it is nice sitting here." I thought it also meant, "It's your turn to say something," so after a few more *mmms* I would ask about his recent fishing trip to Norway, though I happened to know he hadn't caught anything in Norway for some time. He would start to express his disappointment in the fishing there by making a noise that sounded like a cat meowing. "*Eowww,* the fishing is not so good in Norway," and then he would shake his head.

I began to get used to Bengt and our conversations. We had come to what could be called an understanding. There aren't many people you can sit with and not say anything to and still feel as if you're making your point.

Despite our minimalist exchanges I discovered that Bengt liked stories about people having misadventures in the outdoors. City stories about robberies and shootings would only horrify him and reaffirm his resolve to stay as far away from densely populated areas as possible, but anything having to do with a bad reaction between people, the elements, and four-legged creatures got his attention right away.

During one of his visits I told him the tale about the man who tried to stage a photograph of a black bear driving his wife in the family car through Yellowstone Park. The man had spread honey on the steering wheel to lure the black bear into the driver's seat, then instructed his wife to sit in the passenger seat. The husband climbed on top of the hood to take a picture of them through the windshield. After a few frames he instructed his wife to scoot over and put an arm around her furry chauffeur, then watched in horror through the viewfinder as the bear mauled his wife. I told Bengt this story in English with a few Swedish nouns thrown in, but mostly I acted it out. When I got to the part about the bear mauling the woman, and made growling and shrieking sounds, Bengt cracked up.

I also told him about the time I saw a woman get chased off a boardwalk by a buffalo at Old Faithful Lodge. I pantomimed how she had her hands in her pockets as she walked past the buffalo (my index fingers extended out from my forehead, imitating horns) that was grazing next to the boardwalk between the lodge and the gift shop. In a split second the animal charged and took a swipe at her with its massive head.

She didn't even have time to take her hands out of her pockets; she just tipped over the other side of the walkway onto the ground. Lars returned from his phone call in time to find me on my side on the floor with my hands in my pockets and Bengt wheezing with laughter.

I started saving odd stories like this to amuse Bengt. It would help when we grew tired of discussing the weather.

Because Lars is the riverkeeper, most of our visitors are fishermen. Sometimes I didn't hear the knock on the door and found fishermen wandering in the hall, office, or kitchen in stocking feet, looking for someone to sell them a fishing license. After a few polite exchanges in English, we would usually go in search of Lars, with whom they would of course immediately switch to Swedish.

One day we had six visitors in the kitchen, a combination of villagers and fishermen, and like a yawn a sudden silence caught and held the room for a full five minutes. I looked at the floor, at my coffee cup, into the other room. It reminded me of riding in an elevator, except that in an elevator you know your floor will come up, the door will open, and you can get out. In rural Sweden the clock ticks and you wait while people *ja-ha* and *mmm*. And there's this other thing they do when stalling for time or just trying to sound agreeable: they suck in air, as if they've just been doused with cold water, and then say, "*Yooooo*." So the conversation might go something like this:

> SPEAKER: *Vi har mycket mygg i sommar!* (We have many mosquitoes this summer!)
> GROUP RESPONSE: *Ja-ha. Mmm, mmm.*

Then, inevitably, someone will suck in air and go *yoooo*.

This little noise fest goes on until eventually someone raises the next subject.

Most Swedes speak English, though I discovered that the older generation had more difficulties; English was apparently not taught in school when they were young. Sometimes villagers out for a walk would see me practicing my casting or watering flowers in our yard and wave. Sometimes they stopped for a quick chat. Bertil and Gudrun, who live behind us, are retired. They don't speak English, and they know that I don't speak Swedish, but they speak to me in Swedish anyway.

One day, out for his daily stroll to the mailbox, Bertil saw me working in the yard and stopped by for a visit. I knew by the sound of his voice that he was asking me questions. About what, I wasn't sure. I smiled and nodded and hoped I hadn't agreed to baby-sit his grandchildren or let him borrow our car. At any rate, he seemed satisfied with my response and wandered off to get his mail.

I found that if I said, "Hello," people usually shifted the conversation into English. On the rare occasion when I had to interact with someone who did not speak English, I had a few Swedish phrases tucked away. One of them had to do with answering the question *"Var är Lars-Åke?"* (Where is Lars?) To that I would give the well-rehearsed response *"Lars-Åke är nere vid Idsjöströmmen"* (Lars is at the river). Even I became impressed with how authentic I sounded. Trouble was, this convinced them I was fluent, and they would proceed to prattle on in Swedish about various subjects (what subjects exactly, I had no idea). My next response, *"Jag pratar inte svenska"* (I don't speak Swedish), immediately revealed that they had before them a fraud.

"Pratar du inte svenska?" (You don't speak Swedish?)
"Nej." (No.)

I got a lot of quizzical looks from people, but eventually they would make their way down to the river and find Lars.

One day a man arrived in a van, knocked on our front door, kicked off his clogs, and stepped into the kitchen, where I was reading. Swedish laborers wear a kind of one-piece coverall, so I thought he might have just gotten off work and wanted to go fishing. I asked him if he spoke English. He shook his head. Not a word. I had him repeat what he said and listened carefully: *". . . . strömmen . . . klockan tolv till två."* I heard the word for river (*strömmen*) and something about time (*klockan*) between noon and two, and inferred from this that the man wanted to fish the river for about two hours. I replied, smiling, *"Lars-Åke är nere vid Idsjöströmmen."*

He gave me a very confused look and started to back up. I thought this meant he misunderstood me, so I advanced toward him and repeated a little louder, *"Lars-Åke är nere vid Idsjöströmmen!"*

The man looked around frantically, put his clogs back on, and ran out the door, slamming it behind him. *Maybe he didn't understand my accent,* I thought.

When Lars returned three hours later, I asked him about the man I had sent down to the river.

"What man?"

"I sent a man to the river who wanted to fish for two hours."

"I went into Bräcke for the afternoon. Did he pay?"

"No."

"Was he a fly fisher?"

"Um, I don't know."

I had made a terrible mistake. I should not have sent anyone to the river who didn't have a reservation and hadn't paid. I hadn't realized Lars had gone to town on an errand. The last I had heard was that *Lars-Åke är nere vid Idsjöströmmen.* Lars left the house in a rush to see if our visitor had turned our catch-and-release grayling river into an all-you-can-eat fish fry. The man was nowhere in sight.

Later that evening, Lars's son Magnus stopped by to visit. Trying to vindicate myself, I asked him if he knew anything about the man who had been by earlier that day. After all, it is a small village, and he might have seen his car and known him.

"He was driving a blue van and wearing a jumpsuit—you know, the kind workers wear," I explained.

"Oh, that man. He was from the power company," said Magnus.

Lars smiled for the first time since the incident. Then he started to laugh.

"What? What's so funny?" I asked.

He explained that while *strömmen* means "river," it also means "electricity." The man had come to the village to make repairs and wanted to let me know he was turning off the electricity for two hours, to which I had responded by walking toward him with a big smile saying, "Lars is at the river." By his nervous reaction he must have thought I was inviting him in to spend a couple of electric hours with me.

———

I DISCOVERED that a good Swedish hostess needed to know how to make coffee, for expected and unexpected visitors alike. Here was the problem: the kitchen and I were not on speaking terms. Lars was the cook. The last time he had asked me to assist him I enthusiastically reached into the oven with my bare hands to remove a covered casserole that had been baking for over an hour. I had been on leave ever since.

Since Lars prepared all the meals for us, I figured the least I could do was make the coffee. I managed this with some success, although I was always aware that coffee is to a Swede what wine is to a Frenchman, and I sweated each time I brewed.

In Scandinavia coffee gets made in one of two ways: percolated (*bryggkaffe*) or boiled (*kokkaffe*). *Bryggkaffe* is a finer grind, meant for an electric coffeepot. *Kokkaffe* is a coarse grind, which is boiled in a kettle of water, much the way cowboy coffee is made in the West. Theoretically, the loose grounds settle to the bottom of the kettle after boiling. Sometimes, however, the grounds don't settle entirely and spill into your cup when the coffee is being poured, which means they settle at the bottom of your cup and you try not to get a mouthful of them on the last sip.

Either *brygg* or *kok* is brewed and poured morning, noon, and night in Sweden. There is no such thing as decaffeinated coffee. Don't even ask. Yet no one complains about nervousness or restless sleep. Nor does anyone seem to count the calories in the cakes and cookies offered at coffee time: *pepparkakor* (ginger cookies), *prinsesstårta* (marzipan cake), and a delightful variety of sugar cookies.

"Coffee?"

"Yes, please."

Coffee is poured. Treats are produced and displayed on

doily-draped plates—at least that is the idea. Since we lived so far out in the country, we did not get to the grocery store more than once a week. I purchased cookies and *kanelbullar* (a cinnamon bun), intending to have these sweets on hand when visitors arrived, but I ate most or all of them before anyone showed up, meaning that only coffee could be served.

I swear I measured the grounds and the water when I made coffee, but the results seemed inconsistent. Swedes like their coffee *starkt* (strong). I became very aware of the jokes about weak American coffee—"in America they serve a hot drink called 'tea or coffee' "—so I was sensitive to our visitors' potential unease that an American had been put in charge of the one little pleasure of their day. I stood over the brewing coffee and studied it. I could tell if I'd hit or missed by the color and odor. When I erred on the side of weakness, I scrapped the whole thing and started again. When I erred on the side of strength, meaning it had crossed into the bitter zone, I added more water. The process was always stressful.

If my liberated friends in the States could have seen me with a tray full of coffee cups, set on matching saucers with silver coffee spoons placed on each, accompanied by a ceramic milk pitcher and sugar bowl, all nicely laid on top of a hand-hemmed square of fabric, and then watched me carrying it like a good little *hemmafru* (housewife) to a table full of men—they would have gleefully pantsed (a firm downward pull on the trousers) me on the spot, and then would have watched, delighted, while I screamed with laughter, tripped, and launched the tray into thin air. Then they would have high-fived each other as I landed facedown, bare butt up, while hot coffee and coffee accouterments rained down around me.

———

SOMETHING ELSE I have learned when conversing with Swedish visitors: Americans are noisy. We talk all the time. We talk and talk and talk. Living in rural Sweden for several months soon reduces verbal output to the aforementioned *mmms, ja-has,* and air-intake sounds followed by *yooooo.* It took some time, but eventually I got used to quiet conversation, and even to silence—so much so that lively conversation become nothing short of irritating.

But I wasn't completely converted. There were days when I longed for quick-witted, spontaneous American humor. I missed the irreverent way my friends and I teased each other, or the way strangers openly and easily engaged in conversation in public. I like speaking fast and furious and laughing with gusto.

Nonetheless, during my talk retreat in Sweden I learned to listen and watch. For the most part I found my newfound muteness calming. Living in a country whose language I could not speak was like going to an art gallery. Everyone I met, every scene I walked into, became a canvas to study. Staying quiet allowed me to observe my surroundings and the people more carefully. To follow what was being said, I depended on body language and tone of voice for information. It is amazing what you can hear simply by watching. There was also the newfound pleasure of letting people speak in turn. Not interrupting them meant I actually found out what it was they had to say.

So I began to enjoy the unannounced visitor, the thoughtful pause, and the wonderful grace notes of silence floating above a roomful of Swedish guests while coffee spoons clinked against china cups. Mostly, I appreciated that not having something to say did not mean visitors felt compelled to get up and leave.

The Meeting

ONE OF THE FIRST DAYS I ventured into the village of Gimdalen proper was when I went with Lars to empty the trash. Not the most romantic task, but a necessary one nonetheless. Together we wheeled our industrial-sized trash can to the main road for pickup. This required a five-minute walk down the long dirt road that led from our place and past three neighbors' houses. At the main road we met Rolf, who had also brought his garbage.

Rolf is a contractor in his early fifties, and normally wears white socks with his loafers. His regular facial expression is a quirky little smile, as if he is constantly thinking of something funny. I could tell simply by the sound of his voice that he was witty. If we had been schoolmates and sat across from each other, we would have been in trouble all day long. Upon being introduced by Lars, Rolf shook my hand firmly, and though we could not speak directly to each other, I knew immediately that we were friends.

On the way back to the house, Maud and Carl-Åke waved at us. Maud and Carl-Åke were childhood sweethearts. Like most everyone else in Gimdalen, they had lived in the village all their lives. She is a teacher at the grade school five miles away, and he does carpet-laying, painting, and finishing carpentry. Maud's short dark hair frames the face of a thoughtful and friendly person. Carl-Åke's eyes sparkle when he talks and he has a warm sense of humor.

Their two children, who are of Peruvian and Colombian descent, were playing in the front yard. It is nearly impossible to adopt a Swedish child. The state provides for all Swedish citizens, including children whose birth parents are unable to raise them. Therefore couples who want to adopt children must adopt from other countries. It is thus common to see children of color in the arms of their white Swedish parents.

At the first house on the right, a woman of Asian descent mowed the lawn while a man raked up the clippings.

"I thought Bengt lived in that house," I commented.

"That's Bengt's ex-wife and her new husband," explained Lars.

"Well, what are they doing there?"

"Bengt's fishing in Norway."

"So his ex-wife and her new husband are watching his house while he's away on a fishing trip?"

"Yes."

"Is she from Sweden?"

"Bengt met her in Thailand."

A car came into view on the main road. A man waved at us through the rolled down window as he passed. We waved back.

"Who's that?" I asked.

"That's Tord, one of Bengt's brothers. He's married to Bengt's ex-wife's sister."

"So . . . brothers married sisters."

"Yes."

"Really!"

Apparently Swedes didn't have California divorce attorneys or the *hate you forever* gene that kicks in during property and child-custody settlements in the United States. This gave me some comfort: I had yet to see Margit on this visit. We had met that first summer and become friends, enjoying talking and being together. I really liked her, but that was exactly what had me feeling so squeamish. Although Margit and Lars had parted amicably, Margit and I had not yet defined the next phase of our relationship—or if we were even going to have a relationship—and I felt a little timid about running into her without having time to prepare.

As part of our domestic duties that day we drove the thirty minutes to the nearby town of Bräcke, where the grocery stores and banks are located. Wheeling our cart through the bread section I noticed people turned their heads sharply in the direction of my voice when I spoke. When I glanced back at them they looked away. This kept happening. I thought they were listening to my American English, but maybe I was simply too loud. Being a little too loud in Sweden is really only permitted after five in the evening. If you gut-laugh or hoot before then you may be suspected of having a drinking problem; after five in the evening, you're on the safe side of the clock. It's all just a question of timing.

Heading toward the frozen food section, we turned a corner and I almost rammed straight into Margit's sister, Karin. My anxiety meter pegged the red zone. I know sisters because I have a sister. Sisters talk. There was no doubt Karin would report to sister-central that the girlfriend had been spotted. Any details regarding peculiar behavior, extra body fat, odd comments, or bad hair at this sighting would be collected and reviewed. I wanted to bolt for the parking lot and lock myself in the car, but somehow I managed to stand still and crank a smile in place while Lars and Karin exchanged greetings in Swedish.

Karin is a pretty woman with short blond hair. She is a nurse at the community hospital, and has a reputation for being a warm and kindhearted person who loves children. There was nothing to fear, really. After being introduced, she asked me in English how I was, and if my son and I liked living in Gimdalen. I don't remember what I answered. I think I said something like "We're fine and we won't cause any trouble, I promise." Talking with her relaxed the viselike grip my shoulders had on my neck, and by the end of our visit the corners of my mouth had quit twitching and I smiled more naturally. She reminded us that the village pub would be open on Saturday, and said we should come. Lars nodded and told her we'd be there. After we had said our good-byes, I steered the cart toward the candy aisle. I needed chocolate.

———

THE VILLAGE PUB is an old house on the main road that was transformed into a meeting place. Sponsored by the village council, it is run on a volunteer basis and only open a few select nights a year: before the July barn dances and at Christmastime.

The idea behind the pub was to raise money through beer and popcorn sales to build a sauna in the local community center. I'm no math wizard, but it seemed to me that the amount of money and labor necessary to transform the house into a pub should have been more than enough to build a sauna. However, the whole purpose of the pub is to bring people together. No one in the village misses a night at the pub. No one. Baby carriages are parked in front, and kids dash in and out of the building, bumping your elbows, jostling your drink. The place gets filled with people talking and laughing, and the music plays full blast.

I had so far spent most of my time at the house or down by the river, not really meeting anyone outside of fishermen or the closest neighbors. It was time to meet more Gimdalen residents. Considering this was my first official appearance, I applied extra deodorant.

The sound of voices drifted on the cool night air as Lars, Peter, and I headed toward the pub. A large commercial bus, which would transport people from the pub to the barn dance located some thirty-five minutes' drive away, was parked on the main road. Pods of people were gathered outside, beers in hand. Everyone had dressed up. This was clearly a Saturday evening to be treated with some ceremony. A few looked over as we approached—in that subtle way villagers observe things in which they pretend not to have any real interest. Just before we stepped through the pub's doorway, a woman stopped us.

"Hej, Olsson! Hur mår du?"

She seemed jovial, switching to English and teasing Lars about whether he had forgotten his Swedish after living in America all winter. She turned to me and apologized that her English wasn't better.

"How do you like Gimdalen?"

"I think it is beautiful. Very beautiful and I like it very much."

"I lived in the United States for nine months in Boston. I was a nanny for a family there."

Then she leaned closely toward me as if she was letting me in on a big secret.

"You are Lars-Åke's *sambo*. Do you know what *sambo* is?"

"No."

"If you are not married, it is the Swedish word for the person you live with."

"We don't have a word for that in the U.S. We might get ideas, so they don't let us have a word like that."

"I know, not so many Swedes marry like they do in the United States. In Sweden it is very common to have a *sambo*. I have my children with my *sambo,* but it is not the same problems you get for living together as you do in the—"

Someone distracted her and we separated with a friendly nod. Lars took Peter over to a group of kids who quickly included him in a game of chase, then took my hand and walked with me into the pub. A photographer who had taken black-and-white portraits of villagers in various activities—

though moose hunting seemed most prevalent—used the pub as a gallery.

The interior was warm and rustic and a little dark, the walls decorated with rusted farm implements and artifacts, such as saws and axes from the logging days. Nets used for lake fishing hung in one corner over a candlelit table. In front of the bar were several wooden stools that looked as comfortable as a bicycle seat. A dartboard was placed at eye level near the doorway. The minute you stepped over the threshold, a dart whizzed by your head—*thump*—and stuck into a board somewhere near your right ear. Kerosene lamps scented the air.

Sixty or more people must have been crowded into this cozy space. Small groups gathered at tables tucked against the far wall. In another room, off to the side, more people congregated at painted chairs and tables in front of windows that looked out over a potato field. Frank Sinatra singing "The Lady Is a Tramp" was playing on the stereo.

People called to Lars. At me, they smiled or at least stared. But I was too preoccupied about meeting Margit to care.

"I want a beer," I whispered to Lars.

He pushed through the crowd to get one. Alone in a sea of Swedes, I scanned the faces and found her. She and her boyfriend were seated at a table in the corner. Our eyes met. I smiled in recognition and felt my feet move toward her; she stood up from the table and moved toward me. Whether the room swelled with sound or became silent I have no idea.

"Hello," I said.

"Hello," she said.

"How are you?" I continued.

"Good," she answered.

"Good," I answered.

We nodded in unison. Lars returned with my beer. He greeted his former wife with a hug. I found his presence somehow annoying. This wasn't his meeting; it was our meeting—and he was distracting us with idle conversation, shaking a small bowl of beer nuts at us as if we were pets. She refused his offer. I scooped up a few peanuts and got close to his face.

"You need to leave."

Quietly and obligingly, he faded into the crowd. With Lars out of the way Margit and I turned to each other and made small talk. We talked about our children, what they were doing in school and what they had planned for the summer. We didn't touch on anything dangerous, such as our new lives. If our personal stories hadn't intersected at Lars, we might have shared more; for the time being we felt comfortable talking about the weather, about food, about current events, about anything except—men.

We parted with a hug. Eyes that had been upon us quickly went back to the business of looking at shoes or table or ceiling. I made for the door.

Lars was with a small group outside. I slipped up to his left side and felt his arm embrace me. He finished talking, then kissed me on top of my head.

"Is everything fine?" he asked quietly.

"Everything is very fine."

"You want another beer?"

"I want another beer."

The Baking Cottage

I HAVE DESCRIBED MEETING TORA, Lars's former mother-in-law, during my first trip to Sweden, while she baked *tunnbröd*. Sadly, she had recently died. Rumor had it that during his annual inspection after Tora's death, a chimney sweep had found cracks in the brick mortar of her baking house oven and forbidden any further use of it. It would have to be completely rebuilt. Reminiscing about that special first day in Gimdalen brought back warm memories of watching Tora knead the dough by hand, pat it into mounds each the size of a baby's bottom, and roll it into cake-plate–sized circles. Wooden tools had softly thumped against the table as they were pushed over the dough, or exchanged for other tools, or set aside.

Out on a walk one day, I found myself wandering toward Tora's baking cottage. Her widowed husband was still living on the farm, but he was a pensioner, content to watch television, do crossword puzzles, and visit with his children and many grandchildren in the village. I saw that his car was gone. The house looked dark, and the front door—usually wide open—was shut.

I felt like a thief, but I wanted to have a look around, to breathe the aroma that I remembered so fondly. I wanted to find out whether it would reveal the ingredients of *tunnbröd*. Glancing through the window, I could tell the room had been abandoned for months.

Unlatching the door, hoping that I had not been seen, I quickly let myself in. The heavy wooden door, aged and worn, creaked a long terrible creak before I could gently shut it behind me. The sweet smell of birch wood was so faint it might have just been in my imagination.

Tunnbröd is a uniquely northern Swedish bread. I had eaten a steady diet of it since arriving, and my interest in its origins and how it was made had grown. Talking with Lars and Maud, I had learned that many of the farmhouses in Gimdalen once maintained their own baking cottage, but they had long been neglected and their chimneys condemned. The village recently built a modern baking cottage, which anyone is welcome to rent for the day to exercise their baking skills. It has been a great success, and promises to help keep this bread-baking tradition alive.

Tunnbröd and *knäckebröd* have been made for over two

centuries. Historically the milling of the flour took place in the spring and fall, when water levels were high enough to operate the machinery. A bread that would keep was therefore essential. In the early days, *tunnbröd* was made from barley flour, barley being one of the only grains that could grow in the harsh climate of northern Sweden. Today, *tunnbröd* is made with a mixture of grains, including rye and wheat, and often flavored with anise seeds. It can be baked to the dryness of a cracker or to a softer, more malleable texture suitable for wrapping around meats and cheeses. The dryer the bread, the longer it can be stored without going stale.

One of the distinctive characteristics of the cracker form of *tunnbröd,* other than its forever shelf life, is the one-inch hole in its center. The hole made it possible to string the bread on a long pole that hung horizontally from the ceiling of the baking cottage. There the bread was stored to keep it safe from mice and other varmints. Even though no one stores the bread this way any longer, in commercially made *knäckebröd,* the hole remains.

Baking days were limited, since there were so many other farm chores—washing, cooking, child care, cleaning house, and managing the livestock. Every few months, like a quilting bee, women would gather to share the oven and get their baking done. It was work, but it was also pleasure.

To begin, wood had to be gathered and the fire built—it takes almost three hours to get the oven brick hot enough for baking. The fire was built at the front of the oven; unlike fir or pine, birch is a dense wood that doesn't spit out sparks and coals into the room. While the fire heated the oven, the dough was mixed, kneaded, allowed to rise, and then rolled out.

As soon as the fire burned down, the coals were pushed to the back of the oven into a U shape. This shape helped keep the temperature even around the edges of the bread.

A special rolling pin was used once the dough had been flattened. Called a *kavel,* it had row after row of pyramid-shaped points carved into it. When rolled across the surface, it pierced and pinched the dough so that when it baked it remained flat while retaining its distinctive bubbled texture. Should the baker forget to apply the *kavel* before baking, *tunnbröd* dough would rise with abandon and come out looking like a pillow.

Flour, regularly shaken and spread over the table surface, kept the dough from sticking but dusted the air like pollen. Long, soft-bristled brushes swept away excess flour from the flattened tortilla-looking shapes before they were lifted with long flat slats onto the wooden paddle and slipped into the oven. The oven became so hot the bread was almost ready the second it slid off the wooden paddle and hit the shelf.

Because the oven was waist high, the baker could easily retrieve or deposit the bread with the long-handled wooden paddle. On the outside, white chalky paint made the oven look fresh and clean, although scorch marks usually grace the front upper lip, where over the years flames have lapped like hungry tongues. The oven shelf has been darkened by previous fires. During baking, soot from the hearth is transferred to the bread, giving it dark spots and a smoky flavor. The oven's broad chimney carries the sweet smell of birch smoke into the crisp forest air.

On that day, however, there was none of the cheerful activity I had witnessed the year before, when someone had handed me a glass of white wine and a warm, soft, and buttered *tunnbröd,* and I had tasted history. The room was cold and dusty.

I looked at the oven and felt suddenly and very keenly aware that I had no baking skills. The equivalent of a baking cottage experience for me was standing next to my grandmother as a young girl, learning to make ginger and oatmeal cookies. Grandmother read one of her butter-stained recipe cards that asked for a teaspoon of this spice and a tablespoon of that one. I was allowed to cream the sugar and butter by hand. Squeezing the mixture between my fingers, I felt the butter and sugar melting together. A manual eggbeater beat eggs and milk; it had a red handle and two rotating blades. Flour fell like snow through the screen of the old tin sifter into the mixing bowl.

I enjoyed the simple pleasure of baking with my grandmother, perhaps in much the same way that those in this room had grown to love the smell of the fire, the sound of the dough being rolled out, and their mothers and grandmothers quietly chatting while they worked.

Baking had taken place in the cottage for over a hundred years. I held my palm against the front of the old oven. I wish I could have known all the women who had held court here. Now only the cottage remained. The women, who had grown old under its roof, making the bread that had kept them and their families alive, were gone.

Suddenly, the sound of footsteps on the dirt-and-gravel road that ran past the cottage made me dive for the floor beneath the window. Tora's husband was home after all. While my thoughts raced, trying to come up with something to say should he come in, the footsteps faded. I slowly rose up and saw through the window that he was going to collect the mail. It would take him a few minutes to reach the main road, get his mail, then turn and walk back. By the time he had, I had latched the door behind me, crossed the courtyard, and disappeared into the potato field on the other side.

Bräcke

MY FRIENDS who live on ranches in Montana talk about "going to town." This weekly event requires written lists of supplies, most of which will be gotten at the grocery and hardware store. I never experienced "going to town" for the simple reason that I had always lived in one. However, I soon learned that being tucked away in a Swedish village in the middle of a forest meant staying there until we ran out of milk, which if we timed it right, meant every Friday.

Twenty miles away is Bräcke, the nearest town to Gimdalen. It has two grocery stores, a hardware store, the state-run liquor store, System Bolaget, two banks, a post office, a pizzeria, a shoe store, a dress shop, a sporting goods store, and a train station. The children from villages within a twenty-five–mile radius are bussed to the elementary and middle schools located in the center of town. An adult-education school on the outskirts of town offers languages, vocational training, and other course work. There is also a medical clinic for minor injuries and illnesses. For open-heart surgery you'll need to check in at the hospital in Östersund, eighty miles away.

Bräcke is a no-nonsense place. There are no gift shops, notable restaurants, or tourist points of interest. On a hill overlooking the town is a large white rectangular church with a proud steeple and an idyllic graveyard bordered by a coursing stream. Without a famous cathedral, or battlefield, or beach, Bräcke is a place most people just whiz by on their way through the middle of Sweden.

In the 1970s, when complete modernization of the logging industry left many people jobless, Bräcke Commune witnessed a steady stream of people in Volvos piled high with personal belongings heading for Stockholm in search of opportunity. Those who have remained are mostly retirees and people who work for the essential services—banks, grocery stores, schools, etc.—that keep what's left of the community operating.

Bräcke should be an attractive town. It looks out over a large lake called Revsjön; beautiful houses, dating from the turn of the century, grace the shoreline. The buildings and storefronts along the main street, also built in the early 1900s, have striking red rooflines. The centerpiece is an onion-domed cupola. A recent campaign to make improvements brought Bräcke's main street some structural restoration and a sparkling new paint job, but, sadly, without a viable corporation or industry the once prosperous town will be known only by generations of summer cottage dwellers. For now it is a useful pit stop.

Fridays are Bräcke's busiest days. People come in from the surrounding villages to purchase supplies for the coming week. They go about their business at the grocery store, bank, and hardware store. This offered me the perfect opportunity to watch people in their daily lives. When I arrived at the beginning of the summer I could sense the weight of winter just lifting. Spring cannot come fast enough to the northern part of Sweden (which, for Swedes, means anyplace north of Stockholm). After the short days and long nights of winter, light and warmth from the sun are lifesaving. As soon as a spell of warm weather arrives, sweaters are cast off, chairs are pulled out onto the front porch or the lawn, people roll up their sleeves, turn down their socks, and tilt their faces upward, committing themselves body and soul to the experience of warm sunshine. The sun is a long-lost friend that has finally returned. However, until summer is fully under way (sometime around July), warm weather is unpredictable, coming and going, knocking people emotionally backward and forward, depending on the amount of cloud cover or sunshine.

In May, the people of Bräcke wear the effects of a long winter like extra weight. They move slower and talk slower. They are not inclined to outbursts of laughter and are suspicious of anyone who is. Men let their shirts hang outside their pants and have what looks like a permanent three-day growth of beard. Women seem tidier, but many have done desperate things to their hair: too many home perms have made it brittle, like needles on a dry Christmas tree; gelled and spiked, it stands up at the top like the spiny back of a hedgehog; and they use too much red—and I don't mean Lucille Ball red, but wine red. The children emerge from winter having dyed and highlighted their hair as well. And not just another hair color, such as blond or brunette, but Crayola colors like Indigo Blue or Electric Lime. This attack on the hair is very fashionable throughout Scandinavia and northern Europe, but it still feels odd to hand over my Visa card to a store checkout girl with Razzmatazz Red-spiked hair.

While the younger people might dye their hair or get their noses pierced, old age is not celebrated with similar enhancements or adornments. Senior women wear knit caps pulled down tight, their backs humped from osteoporosis, sprigs of hair like cat whiskers sprouting off the upper lip and chin. The old men are gray and thin and the crotches of their pants flap beneath their bony behinds. Americans are possessed by a fear of aging. Plastic surgery is so popular it has even found its way to Bozeman. There may well come a day when we don't know what an eighty-year-old looks like. But for now, estrogen-replacement therapy and face-lifts don't seem to have made it north of Stockholm.

The elderly don't hide at home; they move about town with walkers and canes, like members of a street gang. Brakes and bars, wheels and padded seats—their metallic equipment looks like weaponry, entitling them to stare back at you as if to say, "Get out of my way or you'll get hurt." They have embraced their old-person style; you can see it in their sensible shoes and their consignment store clothes. They wear their age in your face. Their naturalness is so honest that I sometimes found it hard to look at.

Two grocery stores face each other across the town's square. Though both carry similar products, we always go to the one called ICA, short for Inköpscentralerna (Central Grocery Shop). ICA is a collective of individually owned stores that pool their purchasing power to keep costs down. The other grocery store is called Konsum, part of a chain of stores that opened in 1844. Konsum was originally a cooperative grocery store; participating members shared in the profits at the end of the year, but now both stores basically operate the same.

On my rounds through the ICA I tried to understand what my choices were exactly. I asked Lars questions like What is in these tubes? Is this mayonnaise? Is that tuna? Is this skim milk?

I could almost see the thoughts of other customers derail as they turned from their shopping to take a good look at the woman quacking idiotic questions in English. They probably knew that I was the loud American fly fisher who lived in Gimdalen with Lars. Whether they found me irritating or amusing, I had no idea. They stared, looked me over, then went on about their business.

ICA is not a supermarket with entire aisles dedicated to, for example, breakfast cereals or pet food, such as you would find in the States. At ICA you get one or two brands to choose from—and that's it. Sometimes you don't even get a brand name. Certain products are simply labeled as what they are: *mjöl* (flour), *socker* (sugar), *ris* (rice). Limited choices can feel like censorship to an American, but I actually liked not having to think too long about what brand of rice or sugar to buy.

Another place you'll find the locals of Bräcke is in the Konditori, a coffee shop on the main drag. The pastries there are so wonderful that I could salivate just thinking about them. My favorite was *chokladbiskvi,* a chewy marzipan cookie topped with a creamy chocolate mousse, encapsulated in a shell of dark chocolate. And the coffee is full-bodied and hot. After collecting your treat, you sit down in one of the mismatched antique wooden chairs at one of several tables. Shelves tacked to the walls hold books with cracked and frayed bindings; between the shelves normally hang works by a local landscape artist whose enthusiasm for his subject eclipses his ability to paint it. One-armed school desks are available for kids to sit in, drink their juice, and color while their parents read one of the many newspapers left lying around. The Konditori is probably one of the last public places on the planet where you can still smoke indoors. People puff away over their coffee break at the Konditori as if they were living in the 1950s.

As the population of the area had dwindled, the stores in Bräcke closed, one after the other, like lights being snapped off at night. Since my first summer the specialty plumbing supply had gone, then the used-book store, the children's clothing store, and then, worst of all, the gift shop, with its vast selections of candles, colorful woven rugs, place mats, and craft projects. I had shopped there several times and enjoyed the eclectic collection of items on sale. Next to the cash register was a basket of novelty pens, each with the image of a buxom blonde. Tilt the pen and her dress peeled off, revealing her ample figure. Kids would stand at the counter and play with the pens while their mothers shopped. There was also a pen with the image of a man. When you tilted the pen, his swimming trunks scrolled down. It was more comic than provocative, in my opinion. He looked as if he had just stepped out of the shower and was telling you what time he'd be home from work. But now the gift shop, girlie pens and all, had gone the way of other small businesses in the area, taking what might have been left of the town's sense of humor with it.

One of the only shops that didn't provide raw materials or food and was still making a go of it was a women's clothing shop called Lemon's Mode. The clothes were a mixture of styles. A woman in her twenties might find a few things: a T-shirt, or a pair of blue jeans from a Finnish company. But if you're looking for a hipper look—or if you like Liz Claiborne—follow the heart patients to Östersund, where, in addition to the large hospital, there are over thirty-five thousand people and a variety of shops and services to choose from.

With everyone else leaving Bräcke, the citizens left behind don't seem in the mood to trend-set. They need something to wear to teach school, to work at the bank, to answer the phone in a small office. The older crowd wants something easy to get in and out of—tops that button or zip, skirts and blazers to match. Nothing that revealed cleavage.

Considering what was on display in the window—a pleated skirt, a white blouse, and a flowered scarf—I was certain I wouldn't find anything to interest me. I stepped inside and saw that the new spring and summer wear was starting to appear, in the form of a rack of jogging suits, the kind popular in America in the seventies, when aerobics and tennis were the rage. These came in navy blue with white stripes down the side. Jogging suits were still popular—as were clogs. At the gas station I had seen whole families traveling together by car wearing matching jogging suits. On the other hand, I never saw anyone actually jogging in them. They should probably be called "sitting suits," as they seemed to be the uniform of choice for sitting in a car, camper in tow, during the Swedish five-week vacation, when entire families drive cross-country to camp, visit relatives, or sightsee. It reminded me of the way we were put into our pajamas when our parents wanted to catch a late show at the drive-in.

The woman who ran the store asked whether I needed some assistance. I told her that I needed a coat. It was colder in Sweden than I had thought it would be. She showed me the rack of winter coats on sale. Coats with faux-fur–trimmed hoods seem to be the thing. As I sorted through the coats, something caught my eye—a lightweight coat with a removable hood and a drawstring to give it some shape at the waist, a zippered front, and enough room to wear a sweater underneath. To my enormous surprise, it came in two colors, tan and black. I chose tan. The shop owner and I exchanged smiles as I made my purchase.

Bräcke may not be the most exciting place, but I seemed to be making myself at home. *Scary,* I thought to myself as I quietly slipped out the door.

Food

IT WAS MIDMORNING and I was hungry. I opened the refrigerator. Apart from the plastic tub of margarine, nothing looked familiar. Actually, I wasn't even sure it was margarine, because the writing on the lid was in Swedish. I *guessed* it was margarine—it had the right shape and size. I flipped open the lid. Definitely margarine. I could put it on some bread. On the bottom shelf I found a plastic bag of *tunnbröd* folded in quarters.

Next I looked for some milk to go with my *tunnbröd*-and-margarine sandwich. In Sweden milk does not come in plastic gallon jugs; it comes by the liter in wax-paper boxes, which can be neatly stacked on the top shelf of the refrigerator. To open one, you pull out a flap at the top of the box and tear across the dotted line to make a spout, then you pour. To close, you pinch the open ends together and then fold the flap back down. The first few times I opened the milk I ripped a hole bigger than the dotted lines suggested. When I poured, the contents of the box spewed out; more ended up on the table and on my shoes than in the glass.

Orange juice comes in the same kind of box, and so does a thick white milk product called Fil. Fil is very much like buttermilk or unflavored yogurt. It is good on its own or when poured over dry cereal. But for the first few weeks of my life in Sweden, all these boxed liquids made their debut on my clothes and on the floor. Out of kindness Lars finally supplied me with a pair of scissors to snip the dotted lines.

Foods familiar to Americans are also available. American cereal corporations freight Corn Flakes, Honey-Nut Cheerios, and Special-K across the Atlantic, but they have not found a way to compete with the Swedish muesli, a substantial cereal mix you could grain your horse with. Chewy oats, nuts, corn flakes, raisins, dried banana chips, and dates. A half bowl just about soaks up a box of milk. If all the *musli* in Sweden spilled into the Atlantic, you could walk to America on it.

Other foods that are more typically Scandinavian include cheeses. Cheese—from mild to funky—is offered at almost every meal, including breakfast. The breakfast cheese is large, about the size of a brick, and is whittled away at by means of a slicer. It is best when served on warmed bread with blackberry jam, along with a cup of tea. Some traditional varieties, such as tangy *Prästost* (literally, "priest's cheese"), are made from recipes dating back centuries.

I can manage the breakfast cheeses, but after dinner it is common, as it is elsewhere in Europe, to have a cheese and fruit plate for dessert. Robust blue cheeses, goat cheeses, Bries, and Camembert are enjoyed along with grapes, pears, or apples. Coming from Montana, where the choice in cheese is yellow or white, I did not find it easy to adjust to the earthy aromas, spongy textures, and marbled coloration of the cheeses in Sweden. Sadly, in my opinion, they often smelled like old socks. When the cheese plate is offered to me at social functions, I force myself to make a thin smile, then pass the plate along.

Even though Swedish foods might fall under the general category of continental cuisine, there are some dishes uniquely Swedish, most of which include wild game, that I grew fond of. I also liked everyday fare like *kåldolmar,* which is made of ground meat and rice rolled in cabbage leaves and served with lingonberry (a tart red berry similar in taste to a cranberry) jam. Another traditional weekday meal consists of pancakes and pea soup. This is usually served with a little nip of Punsch, which is a syrupy rum-type drink. *Pytt-i-panna,* which translates to "pieces in the pan," is a hearty skillet meal that consists of potatoes, beets, fried egg, and cubed meat.

Because we lived in the forest country, we were able to get moose meat from the village hunting team, and from Lars's son Fredrik, who is a keen and successful hunter, we received gifts of roe-deer steaks, duck, and woodcock. Occasionally we fished the lakes near our home for perch and pike. We hardly ever had beef because it was very expensive and not that common, though we did buy some reindeer, a rich, flavorful meat.

In the specialty fish category is gravlax, salmon that is cold cured by marinating it in a special mixture of salt, sugar, white pepper, and dill. Gravlax is cut into thin slices and can be served on *knäckebröd* topped with caviar or sweet mustard, usually as an hors d'oeuvre or starter. I soon acquired a taste for *strömming*, or herring. I like it fried or marinated; it is especially tasty when paired with a good aquavit.

Morklor is a dark-brown–colored mushroom found in the late spring. It has a nutty flavor and is great served with moose or reindeer. One afternoon in early June, Ida, Lars's niece, who lived just down the dirt lane from our house, showed up at our door with a shopping bag full of *morklor* she had picked fresh from the forest. We paid her two hundred kronor (about twenty dollars) for the lot, which was a bargain, considering how difficult it can be to find them. The long-legged teenager counted her money, then skipped all the way home.

There is something else worth mentioning about *morklor*. They are highly poisonous. You have to boil them for fifteen minutes—not a minute less—to be free of danger. Lars double-boils them, just in case. In all, it takes three or more hours to clean and remove the stems, then boil and boil them again, then rinse, bag, and put them in the freezer. Lars might begin processing the mushrooms after dinner and be up until midnight boiling and bagging. *Morklor* have enough of a reputation for being dangerous that some guests, when informed we are serving it, push it to the side of their plate. They're nervous about reports that this mushroom might surprise you, something like a bus jumping a curb. I was a bit cautious as well. I always let Lars take the first bite.

When I got homesick and thought about a hot dog or

hamburger I got even more homesick. The Swedish hot dog, *varm korv* (warm sausage), doesn't even come close. It doesn't plump up when you cook it, for starters. No smoky, salty, wonderful flavor to disguise the unmentionable parts. *Varm korv* is long and thin, and even ketchup can't disguise how tasteless it is.

Sometimes, when people found out I was American, they liked to tease me: "Ha ha ha. You from America, I bet you want a hamburger. Ha ha ha."

"Yeah," I responded, "Ha ha ha. But not the kind you have in this country. Ha ha ha."

I'm not sure what hamburgers are made of in Sweden— I think there must be some kind of filler in the patties—they don't taste like beef at all. Someone once gently explained to me that a good amount of horse meat gets mixed in with the beef. I would have been more disturbed by this had I not already seen horse meat, which is considered a delicacy in Sweden, for sale at the grocery store. Whatever they contain, Swedish hamburgers don't look right. They're not dark enough, either on the outside or on the inside. Actually, the meat is kind of white, which goes along with my observation that white is the most common food color in Sweden: potatoes, pork, fish, pancakes, *tunnbröd,* herring, butter, milk. No question about it: Swedes eat a lot of white food.

There really are lots of great flavors and foods in Sweden, yet often I felt stranded when I stood at the refrigerator, its door open wide, hoping to see something I wanted to eat. I saw the tubes of salted caviar that were meant to go on eggs and *knäckebröd*. I smelled a strong blue cheese that Lars had left half-wrapped; there were salad greens, apples, and some carrots. I couldn't seem to find what I was looking for. What *did* I want? I wasn't sure. There was bread and fruit and vegetables, milk and yogurt. But everything came in different packaging and was labeled in a different language. I wanted something . . . familiar, something I didn't have to translate. I wanted a Montana beefsteak, a baked Idaho potato topped with butter and sour cream from Wisconsin, served with a tossed green salad and ranch dressing from California. My taste buds were homesick. Until I could get them back across the ocean, I was always going to be a little bit hungry.

I took the *tunnbröd,* margarine, and milk out of the refrigerator, then closed the door.

Midsummer

BERTIL AND GUDRUN, the retired neighbors who lived behind us, were busy in their yard pruning, watering, and mowing. Then they disappeared into the forest. Somewhat later they returned, looking like walking trees, their faces obscured by a waving mass of long birch branches that they had cut. They marched the greenery to their front porch and began lashing the branches to the porch posts. Soon I noticed they were arranging lawn furniture and tilting table umbrellas, so they could drink their coffee without getting the morning sun in their eyes.

The entire village was a little more animated than usual. I heard the drone of lawn mowers and the voices of children at their games. Down the road I saw Maud, standing on her front porch, shaking and snapping the dirt and dust from a rug. A beautiful folk dress was hanging out to air. The weather forecast promised a warm, sunny day. This had put everyone in an extremely good mood. But the activity also had to do with something else. It was Midsummer.

Celebrated on the weekend closest to the summer solstice, Midsummer marks the turning point from the longest hours of daylight to the shortest. During pagan times, throughout various parts of Europe, Midsummer's Eve was a night for rejoicing and merrymaking. Because days grew shorter after the solstice, there was fear that the sun might not come back. Bonfires were lit to help drive away evil and to encourage the sun to rise again.

Midsummer is also traditionally a time for lovers. In Sweden, it is said that by picking seven different wildflowers and putting them under her pillow on Midsummer's Eve, a woman will dream of the man she will marry. It is a popular weekend also for weddings; consequently scores of anniversaries are celebrated. The birch branches Bertil and Gudrun had put up were a traditional decoration—a summer version of the Christmas wreath. It is a time for people to don their folk dress and wear crowns of woven wildflowers.

In Gimdalen, out-of-town guests and family were expected to arrive by the tens and twenties, swelling the village's population to nearly two hundred. Lars's family members had arrived the evening before, after a seven-hour drive from their home in the south. Eva, Lars's mother, a diminutive, vivacious woman with dark hair and brown eyes, was already busy baking bread, cooking, and generally making the kitchen her home away from home. Christina, Lars's sister, a life transitions counselor, is a lively woman who has inherited her mother's energy. She came bearing gifts of curtains, candles, and dishes to brighten the house. Lennart, Christina's husband, is a tall, slender, and dark-haired man; he works for an international transportation company. A man of few words, Lennart quietly negotiated his way through the flurry of activity his wife and mother-in-law generated. Our little house was soon noisy with the conversation and laughter of people on holiday.

Before Lars's family arrived, there had been a great deal of discussion about what food and wine would be served and how the table would be set. I learned that this same discussion was taking place in kitchens around the village. Swedes are generally very enthusiastic about visiting relatives. They don't grumble about cooking and cleaning, or feel put upon by holidays in any way. In fact, they can't wait for the party to get started.

One sure way to get things going is to have on hand a variety of wines and spirits, so everyone makes a visit to System Bolaget. Indeed, before every major holiday, villagers from Gimdalen and other outlying villages gather at System Bolaget. The store turns into the town square. You see just about everyone, giving you a chance to exchange information about who's visiting for the holiday, or whether you will be going out of town to stay with relatives or friends. At System Bolaget in Bräcke, the wines and spirits are displayed in locked glass cases, and a catalog lists all the other offerings. You write the numbers that correspond to your choices on a slip of paper, then wait in line. When it's your turn, you step up to the counter and hand over your order. The clerks go to the storage area in the back, bring out your bottles, then stack them in bags or boxes for you to carry away. It is all amazingly orderly.

Our Midsummer dinner took place in the early afternoon. The friendly takeover in the kitchen engineered by Eva and Christina, left me with the task of setting the table. I put out plates, silverware, and cloth napkins, then took scissors to the wildflowers I'd picked near the barn and created a large centerpiece of "priest collars," as the Swedes call daisies, buttercups, yarrow, woodland geranium, and red campion. Lars and Lennart lit the grill—manfully preparing to barbecue the marinated *fläskfilé* (pork steaks). Christina opened glass jars of *inlagd sill* (spiced herring in vinegar and onion) and forked the contents into oblong crystal herring dishes paired with silver plates. Dishes of sliced pickled beets, boiled new potatoes from the village, chopped onion, and—of course—*knäckebröd* were arranged on the table. Aquavit and beer glasses were placed next to the water and wineglasses.

As soon as everything was ready, Lars called us to the table. All of us, including Peter, had changed clothes for the occasion—dresses for the women, ties and jackets for the men. The formality felt right.

An aquavit sampler with twelve different types was opened and passed around. Everyone examined each label, and a lively discussion followed about which brand to try first. Aquavit (literally, "water of life") is flavored vodka, different spices and aging processes creating each flavor. Some aquavits are fruity, hinting of orange or apple; some have the more medicinal taste of juniper. There are many brands, such as

Skåne, Herrgårdsakvavit, and Gammal Norrlandsakvavit. I thought one in particular, called Beska Droppar, tasted like the cough syrup I took when I was a kid. The one I decided to try first was Rånäs, which is based on an old recipe that was coming back in fashion.

I was instructed to take my fork and spear a piece of herring, along with a piece of beet, a piece of potato, and a piece of onion, and put it all on top of a piece of buttered *knäckebröd*. Shot glass full of aquavit in one hand, herring sandwich in the other, we listened while Lars made a toast. He spoke about how great it was to be together, how beautiful the weather, how wonderful the day, and then he finished with the familiar salutation *Skål*. First we took a bite of our herring sandwiches, then we tossed back a swallow of aquavit. Flavors of clove, beet, potato, fish, and the sharp clean bite of aquavit burst in our mouths. This was a much-loved part of the meal, a ritual that brought back warm memories of Midsummers past. We continued to sip and sample the other aquavits and ate more *knäckebröd* and herring. Finally we rose from the table and went out to the yard to sit while Lennart and Lars ran the grill.

The sound of lawn mowers had ceased, but voices were carried along on the gentle breeze. We could see that Bertil and Gudrun's children and grandchildren had arrived; they were crowding around tables that had been set up outside. Grills were going throughout the village. Charcoal-brick–scented smoke wafted through every yard. On the front lawn of a house across the main road was a long table set with china, linens, and vases of wildflowers. Twenty people sat there enjoying their Midsummer feast; for hours we could hear their chatter and laughter.

Soon the fillets were cooked and our dinner commenced. In addition to the pork, there were more boiled new potatoes, warm French-cut beans, one of Lars's delicious sauces for the meat, green salad, and Eva's bread. The aquavit was put aside and three types of red wine were served. For dessert there was *chokladtårta* (chocolate layer cake) and, naturally, strong coffee.

Conversation switched from English to Swedish and back. It was easy to tune in or tune out, depending on the subject. Eva gave Peter some Swedish words to practice, Christina and I spoke in English, Lars and Lennart conversed in Swedish, and then Lars and Lennart would speak to me in English, Eva to Christina in Swedish, both of them to Peter in English. Breathing in one language, exhaling another, on and on we rambled.

An hour later, Bertil, Gudrun, and their family walked past our window, giving us a wave as they went by. The man who lived across the field from us left the house with his visiting relatives. It was time to head for Kullagården, the community gathering place, where everyone was invited to join in decorating and raising the Midsummer pole. We soon followed.

The wooden Midsummer pole is a giant cross about twenty-five feet high, with loops that hang off the ends of the crossbeam, like a pair of earrings. The pole is stored in a barn all year and brought out only for this occasion. It is laid on the ground, so that people can attach the grasses, flowers, and greens they have picked to its frame. This means that by the time the Midsummer pole is ready it is very heavy with decorations; several men are required to lift the thing into position. They hoist the Midsummer pole off the ground and push it the rest of the way up, looking eerily like those Marines raising the flag on Iwo Jima. Once the pole is in place, it is greeted with applause.

Maud, who knows the words to all the traditional songs, encouraged children to come forward to dance and sing around the Midsummer pole. She wore a folk dress that she had woven and stitched herself. Every region in Sweden has a particular style, pattern, and color of folk dress. Some villages have their own design as well. Gimdalen's dress is a rust-colored vest, buttoned down the front and fitted over a white blouse. A rust-colored shawl is pinned at the chest with a heavy, ornate silver pin. The midcalf-length skirt, pleated at the waist, has a rust-and-dark-blue–striped weave. A leather pouch hangs off the right hip, and to complete the ensemble, dark knee-high stockings are paired with low-heeled black shoes that sport big silver buckles.

Maud managed to gather a group of children and their mothers. I couldn't resist. Peter and I joined hands with the group of twenty or so. The dance began. We walked in one direction and then back the other way as we moved through the songs. One song sounded like "Old MacDonald Had a Farm," and involved various animal noises that made everyone laugh. During another song we started off walking slowly, then ended up at a full gallop. Another had us swinging our arms forward and stepping toward the pole, then out again. The rest of the Midsummer revelers stood by, smiling and enjoying the scene. As we spun through yet another folk song (this one had us circling the Midsummer pole at dizzying speed) I thought *how lucky we were*. How wonderful it was to be in a place where celebrating the sun brought so many people home to hold hands and to sing.

Barn Dance

SATURDAY NIGHTS IN JULY are barn-dance nights. Villages throughout northern Sweden host dances with live music in large outbuildings or in reconfigured barns. It was explained to me that even a hundred years earlier people in the countryside went to these kind of dances as a way to meet people from other villages—similar to the western schoolhouse dances, or those dances held in Montana during frontier times, when people gathered after haying or shipping cattle. The reason was the same: because of the distance between ranches, social occasions were often the only time you could meet a potential spouse. The barn-dance tradition lives on in the forest country of Sweden and is a much anticipated part of summertime fun. Gimdalen doesn't have the facilities for a barn dance, so they hire a tour bus to get them to one. The dances start at nine in the evening, and to help loosen up everyone's two left feet, there is the Gimdalen pub.

The first dance of the season was being held in the village of Storåsen, twenty miles away. Lars and I walked down to the pub for a beer—and to see what was going on. Because the pub is not a commercial operation, the only way you can find out when it will be open is by reading the announcements in the Bräcke community flyer, or by seeing the carved wooden sign that simply reads *Öppet* (open) when it appears on the main road. By the time we got there, half an hour after opening, the place was crowded. Everyone was there: grandmothers, aunts, couples, teenagers, and people from other villages. The usual assortment of bicycles, cars, and baby carriages were parked outside the door. The men had shaved and combed their hair.

Children, including my son, who was spending the night at a friend's house, ran in and out of the building, bumping into the legs of people who, though it was early in the evening, were already having difficulty steadying themselves. It all felt like a wedding reception, the kind of free and easy atmosphere in which your parents tell jokes you never heard them tell before, your grandmother laughs a little louder than usual, you see your aunt sneaking a cigarette around the corner. Couples kissed openly and often. People mingled on the lawn next to the road; their voices and laughter could be heard from one end of the village to the other.

We got our beers and accepted an invitation from our neighbors, Carl-Åke and Maud, to sit with them.

"Are you going to the dance?" they asked.

I looked at Lars.

"I don't think so," he replied.

I looked back at our neighbors.

"Maybe," I offered.

Our neighbors looked at Lars and chuckled. We talked about fishing, the weather, how I liked living in Sweden, and we had another beer. Someone turned up the volume on the stereo. Sven-Bertil Taube, a famous Swedish folksinger, was singing *"Flickan i Havana"* ("The girl from Havana").

Yngve, a man well known locally for his black currant wine, invited us to follow him to his car. He opened his trunk and produced a screw-cap wine bottle—the label scratched off—and poured us a sample of its purple contents into plastic drinking cups. Yngve is a trusted vintner in the village who makes annual batches of sweet wines from black currant berries. He likes people to taste his wines. If you like them he might give you a bottle. It tasted sweet and earthy—like wet dirt. With lips pressed together I mustered a tight smile and nodded. Lars told him it was better than last year's. He poured us another sample. We sipped and nodded and smiled. When we had finished, he closed the trunk, looking very pleased, and walked off.

It began to rain. The revelers moved under the eaves of surrounding buildings or indoors. By eight o'clock there were over seventy people. Some were deep in conversation at corner tables. One man walked through the crowded room, full beer glasses in each hand, looking for someone he had apparently lost. Near the entrance, several men gazed shamelessly at women as they passed by. Women normally seen hanging wet laundry or stooping over a potato field wore eye shadow and lipstick. Coyly glancing about the room, they occasionally burst into spasms of flirtatious laughter.

Children continued to run in and out, although the rain had brought most of them indoors to ask for money for popcorn and soft drinks. They then lined up in front of the bar, which was a very thick and ancient log that had been sawed in half, and pressed their kronor onto its wooden surface. The man who waited on them cranked off the caps of their bottled Fantas or Pommac (a kind of Swedish ginger ale); the smell of popcorn filled the air.

At nine o'clock the bus arrived and began to fill up. The pub emptied until only our table was left. Our neighbors rose to leave.

"Lars, I want to see this. Let's go to the dance."

Lars hesitated. The neighbors encouraged.

"Come on," I cajoled. "I've never been to a barn dance before."

There are people who like to dance and people who do not. Lars is not particularly fond of dancing, although he did once tell me he had won a New Year's dance contest dancing the Charleston.

The next thing I knew, Lars and I were trying to find a seat on the bus to Storåsen. I found a seat in front, Lars one in the back. The bus was one of those large modern touring ones and we looked like a chartered group of sight-seers, laughing as it roared over the dirt road through the forest, consuming go-cups of beer and sips of the moonshine that was being discreetly passed between seats.

A man decided to use the stairway at the front of the bus

as a conductor's pit. He took out a comb wrapped in wax paper and began to buzz out a folk tune. He waved his hands, trying to lead the passengers in song, then lost his balance and stumbled down the stairs. But he bounced back up, laughing and singing and trying to encourage the passengers to sing along. The bus driver didn't seem fazed by this; neither did the rest of the passengers. People smiled and shouted out requests. At every turn in the road the man fell back down the stairs, but he always came bouncing back up, buzzing tunes on the comb.

At one point the driver pulled the bus over to the side of the road. As far as I could tell we were in the middle of nowhere. Half the passengers started to get off the bus. I thought the man playing the comb would get trampled, but he must have been the first one out the door. Lars filed past me.

"Do you have to pee?" he asked.

"What?"

"Get out and pee," he said, before being pushed down the aisle and out the door.

I looked out the window. The women dashed into the woods to find a tree to hide behind. The men crossed the road and stood elbow to elbow, like a chorus line, their backs to the bus. Soon everyone had returned to his seat and we were on our way.

Twenty minutes later, we arrived. Four other tour buses were already there, and as soon as the doors opened we were hit by the sound of live music pulsating from across a meadow. A crowd of people stood outside the large square building where the dance was being held. People had come from miles away.

It had been raining off and on that evening and the air

was unusually humid. Lars took my hand and we walked toward the source of the music. People talked and laughed and looked each other over. There must have been more than three hundred. Every age was represented: middle-aged women in skirts and sandals, young men with spiked hair and leather jackets, teenage girls in tight pants and glittery eye shadow, plump retired couples, elderly men with a mischievous glint in their eyes.

The building had one large open wall with sliding doors, letting in lots of air and allowing people to move in and out of the dance area easily. There was a snack bar, where women served coffee and soda and made sandwiches. No alcoholic drinks were served; if you wanted to imbibe, and people did, you had to sneak in your own supply or get yourself invited to someone's car, where moonshine or beer was available. We stepped through the entrance just as the band was taking a break. People scattered toward parked cars or walked behind the building for a smoke. Security guards looked the other way, I was told, so long as there were no fights and people made an effort to keep their bottles and cans out of plain sight. Lars suggested I sit with the women.

"What?"

"Over there. The women are on that side of the room. The men stay on this side of the room."

He was right. A majority of the women were on the right side of the room and the majority of men were on the left side of the room. The women stood in small groups, checking their hair and makeup in compact mirrors, passing around breath mints, and carefully looking over the men in attendance. I felt like I was at a prom.

"What am I supposed to do over there?" I asked.

"Wait for someone to ask you to dance," Lars answered.

"I'll wait here," I said, holding his hand more firmly.

The music began again. People gravitated toward the dance floor and began to do a simple cheek-to-cheek, cha-cha-cha-like shuffle, exactly what I had seen on the *Lawrence Welk Show*. The dancers moved counterclockwise around the room. I continued to hang on to Lars's arm.

"I can't dance this dance," I shouted into Lars's ear.

"What?"

"Are they going to play any rock? I can dance to rock."

"No. You must learn. It is the fox-trot. Watch what people are doing. It's easy."

The band played their version of the ABBA song "Dancing Queen." There was a drummer, bass guitar, lead guitar, keyboard player, and a barefoot female vocalist who both sang and shook a tambourine. She was on the chubby side, but still sexy, I thought. She wore thin white cotton pants tied in front with a drawstring and a loose-fitting gauzy top that exposed her belly; her long blond hair flowed loosely with her movements. She also played the accordion. The band members all had microphones and synchronized their vocals to the various songs. Every now and then one of them stepped on a peddle, releasing a cloud of fog that floated across the stage floor. Colored stage lights flashed to the beat.

The music was a mixture of folk dances, polkas, and various versions of (inevitably) ABBA and Beatles' songs. People danced past us like fish swimming in an aquarium. Middle-aged women danced with young men, young women danced with young men, married men danced with single girls, married people danced with other married people. Bodies jiggled, sensible shoes shuffled, people smiled. Every other song, dancers switched partners—unless, some kind of relationship was brewing. The fourth song in the set ended, and a sign that read *Herrarnas* lit up over the bandstand and started flashing.

"Men's choice," Lars explained. "The men ask the women to dance. When the other sign that says *Damarnas* is lit, then it is the women's turn to ask for a dance."

"Good. Ask me to dance then."

"No. Someone else is going to ask you."

"I don't want to dance with . . ."

A tall man had approached me, bowed, and asked in English if I would join him for the next set. Lars grinned and pressed the palm of his hand against my lower back. How could I say no? After all, the man *had* bowed.

Off we went. It quickly became obvious to the man that I was having a little problem with the fox-trot. He let me practice with my arms up in proper dance position, my head hung low to get a good look at our feet. I felt like his younger sister. "One, two, one—one, one, two—," I counted out loud, trying not to step all over the poor man. Soon the dance floor became so crowded that keeping step didn't really matter anymore—we all sort of bumped into each other, and the motion of moving toward and away from each other became the dance. It became warm, I was sweaty . . . it was the next song. My dance partner seemed not to mind that I couldn't follow him. He was kind enough to smile and tell me I danced fine. I wished the band would play some Doobie Brothers.

After the second song, I was politely deposited back on the bench next to Lars, who gave me a ridiculously pleased-looking grin. Suddenly the *Damarnas* sign started to flash. Women darted to the men's side of the room and whisked men off to the dance floor. A full-figured woman approached Lars. He accepted, she embraced him, and away they went, fox-trotting around the room like a newly wound clock. I was impressed.

At the beginning of the next set a man in his seventies came to collect me. I attempted desperately to dance a stress-free fox-trot, trying to make myself light and limber in his arms. Despite my clumsiness he made me feel as if I was in step. He loved to dance. After two sets he thanked me before depositing me on the bench.

Then began a folk dance called the Hambo, in which partners step, skip, and twirl in perfect precision. At one point the dancers stomped in unison and the whole room vibrated. Brothers danced with sisters, husbands with wives, granddads with granddaughters. It was energizing just to watch. When the Hambo finished, the band took a break. Lars and I went outside for air.

People were walking or standing on the lawn in front of the building or in the surrounding meadow. A group of James Dean impersonators leaned against the building or ran fingers through their hair. Some stood with their hands in their pockets, others tucked a pinch of snuff under their upper lip; they all eyed the girls that walked by. Women reapplied lipstick, sprayed shots of cologne on their necks, and ate breath mints. Off in the distance I saw a young man supporting his date while she hung her head over some shrubbery. The music began again and the crowd congealed back onto the dance floor.

People fox-trotted or practiced a mild version of the jitterbug and we all worked up a pretty good sweat. I started to feel a little nauseated from the smell of stale booze on people's breath and the smell of cigarette smoke on clothes and hair. While I rested, people swirled past me in various stages of bliss or exhaustion. A red-faced man, looking as if he might be having a heart attack, was draped over the shoulder of a woman twenty years younger and thirty pounds thinner. They shuffled around the room as if he were a cabinet. I could see her expression of tolerance. Another couple slow-danced with their eyes closed despite the fast beat of the music. They were either in love or asleep.

The next-to-last dance was upbeat and fast. People were in such a frenzy to catch the last few minutes of the evening that it could have been New Year's Eve. We bumped into each other and waved at neighbors and smiled at friends and exchanged knowing looks over the intoxicated couple that kept tripping and jostling into other dancers.

The last dance was a slow dance. Only those who were either in some kind of real relationship or desperately wanted one to begin with a new partner stepped onto the floor. The others watched or made preparations to leave. Lars and I danced. It felt sweet and pleasant and uncomplicated. He held me firmly by the waist and moved me effortlessly around the dance floor. "Do you come here often? Can I take you home?" he asked, then kissed me and demanded to have my phone number.

At one in the morning the dance ended. People stepped onto the Gimdalen-bound bus warm and sleepy-eyed, hair undone, shirts opened at the neck, makeup faded. The man with the wax paper comb was fast asleep in a front seat. The flasks of moonshine were empty. Back at the village, the doors opened in front of the pub and a subdued crowd filed quietly out. The rain had stopped; a cool evening breeze freshened the air. I thought about the generations of people in that part of the world, dancing rhythmically, like heartbeats, at barn dances over the centuries. I was determined that by the end of July I'd have the fox-trot figured out.

Familjegraven

"WE'RE GOING to visit the family graves tomorrow."

Lars made this announcement while I was washing the dinner dishes. Eva, his mother, who was visiting us, continued to clear the table. All evening they had been speaking only in Swedish, and I apparently had not caught any of the words for "grave," "church," or "flowers." If I had, I might have had time to put it all together, think, and come up with an excuse not to join them. I pictured tears, hand-holding, tissues. *Why had they come up with this idea?* The sun had been shining, the wildflowers were in bloom, and a slight breeze kept mosquitoes at bay. I decided to play it Swedish. I remained silent and placed a dish on the drying rack.

"My sister took Mom last year," explained Lars. "Mom liked it very much. I haven't been to my father's grave for many years and I'd like you to see it. It's in Långsele, the town where I grew up. We want to show it to you. It will be like meeting the rest of my family."

I rinsed the last dish, then pulled the sink plug and let the water drain. Eva and Lars stopped talking and waited for my answer.

Långsele is two hours northeast of Gimdalen. Lars, Eva, and I drove along back roads through countryside that had been prosperous when logging had created a booming economy and steady work. Today the majestic houses we drove by, once the pride of the Jämtland, looked like patients in a rest home waiting for someone to come visit. As we drove along, in my mind I straightened and reroofed the houses, painted them, and moved families in.

We crossed over bridges spanning rivers where loggers had guided timber to the mills hundreds of miles away. No longer.

"It was a hard life," said Lars.

Logs had jammed and crushed strong men or spun them off into cold dark waters. The rivers had taken their share. Plucked them here and there like berries.

The rains had greened the forest. Lupine, fireweed, daisies, pansies, wild rose, and clover painted the meadows and lined the moist roadside ditches. In Gimdalen we brought armfuls of these wildflowers into the house and arranged them in old teapots, milk pitchers, and vases. We passed a mother and daughter gathering flowers near their *sommarstuga* (summer cottage). Seeing the women reminded Eva that she wanted to stop at the grocery store when we got to Långsele. She wanted to buy refrigerated hybrid roses wrapped in pink paper for the graves. Field flowers—weeds, technically—would not do.

Långsele, in an area known as Ångermanland, has nearly a thousand inhabitants. Formerly a mighty salmon river, Fax-älven runs through the middle of it. Downstream from Lång-sele is the larger town of Sollefteå, where a college, hospital, military headquarters, and shopping make it a center for the outlying communities. Once a major rail transfer station for passengers heading farther north, Långsele used to be a thriv-ing concern. People don't travel by train the way they used to, however, and like the rest of northern Sweden, the town has suffered a steady decline.

Lars's parents were born and raised near Långsele, and so were he and his sister, Christina. His mother and father had attended the same school together, married, and made a life for themselves, with Eva taking care of the children and Ture working for the railroad. Along the banks of Faxälven the family had picnicked, fished, and hunted; in the winter they cross-country skied. Lars remembers a happy childhood. He remembers the skiwear his mother sewed for him; he remem-bers his father waxing his skis and offering encouragement before competitions. Lars talked often of the time they spent camping and fishing, always the four of them, working and playing together. His parents were demonstratively affection-ate. They were not wealthy by material standards, but emo-tionally they were millionaires. When Lars was fifteen and Christina eight, Ture suddenly died.

We stopped at the grocery store for flowers, then drove over the bridge that spans the sparkling waters of Faxälven. Lars told me proudly that in 1914 the largest salmon ever caught in Sweden was caught in Faxälven. It weighed nearly eighty pounds. Today there are no more salmon in Faxälven. Hydroelectric dams have been built up and down the river system, putting an end to the runs. I nodded in appreciation and stared longingly at the river as we followed the road on its winding path up the hill to the church and graveyard.

The church was very plain—large, white, and rectangular. We tried the massive double doors but they were locked. The large side windows were too high to look through, even standing on tiptoe. A small side chapel looked more intimate, and Lars and Eva headed toward it. The chapel's big black oval door was also locked.

Eva told me that Ture's funeral had been held in this building. She showed me where she had been standing when she saw her husband's casket for the first time. Flung open, the black doors seemed as if they would swallow her. When she saw the casket near the altar, she had panicked and did not want to enter the chapel. She showed me how she had her right hand over her heart and, knees bent, how she had swooned before relatives caught her and carried her in. Eva stared quietly at the locked door, shook her head, and walked away.

The graveyard was laid out to the north of the church and chapel. The grounds were as beautifully manicured as a putting green. Gravel pathways bordered the grave sites. You could hear each step being taken. Nursery-raised marigolds, pansies, and begonias had been planted near the headstones earlier that summer. I liked seeing the flowers. *People still cared,* I thought.

Lars and Eva walked toward Ture's grave. I passed a small workstation with a sink, where you could arrange flowers, cut them, or wash the dirt from your hands. It also had rakes and a supply of plastic containers with spiked bases, so that flower arrangements could be stuck directly into the ground. Next to the station was a large bin where dead flowers and plants could be disposed of. A sign above it read *Kompost. This whole place is compost,* I thought, smiling.

Marigolds and pansies were planted in front of Ture Olsson's mauve-colored headstone. Eva sent money every year to her sister-in-law, who lived in the town and took care of the grave sites. There were others belonging to Lars's grandfathers, grandmothers, uncles, and aunts. I thought about how they were all here—in one place. I really would be meeting the rest of the family.

Ture had been only thirty-nine when he died. Lars keeps a black-and-white portrait of his father in his office. You can see from the photo that something was wrong. Ture looks thin, and there are dark circles under his eyes. He had a bad heart and was supposed to have had surgery to correct the problem. Just before he left for the Stockholm hospital where he was scheduled for a heart operation he came down with pneumonia. After that cleared up he came down with a bad cold. He didn't want to miss his scheduled operation at the hospital, so he traveled on the train to Stockholm in hopes that his cold would clear up and he could still be operated on. It was winter. He died at the hospital before they could help him. Eva became a widow at thirty-five.

We stood over Ture's grave in silence. Lars took the flowers from me and started to arrange them in one of the plastic vases.

Eva usually moves and speaks with great vitality. She is quick-witted and bright. When she talks about something that strikes her as funny, her story and her laughter gain momentum until she starts to lose her breath and has to squeeze her words out in a high-pitched squeal. This in itself is hilarious, and she'll go on squealing until we are all laughing so hard tears run down our cheeks.

Eva gazed over the rest of the cemetery. She was looking, she said, for the grave of Kurt Olsson, the husband of Ture's sister (the woman who tended the graves). He had died three years earlier, and the sister-in-law had complained about Eva's not coming to the funeral. Recalling this brought on a discussion of this particular sister-in-law, who never visited, never wrote, and only called when someone in the family had died. Eva remarked that this woman had also criticized her for the way she raised her children after Ture died. Lars translated for me while Eva's voice grew louder and her monologue became fraught with irritation. Suddenly switching into English, she said, "Kurt was such a nice man," and with that she turned and walked off to look for his grave.

We spread out and begin to roam through the cemetery, reading out grave markers as if looking for an address in an unfamiliar neighborhood. Per Andersson 1904–1960, Emil Bergström 1878–1958, Nils Nilsson 1884–1945, and his wife, Anna 1885–1980, Jenny Persson 1901–1975, and Lilla Monika 1958–1959. I worked out the math of their ages, but wanted to know more. Shouldn't something else have been etched in the stone? Death suddenly seemed very frightening. It reduced life to the simple letters that formed our name and the dates of our existence. Surveying the cemetery I also noted that for the most part the stones and markers were evenly situated; one didn't rise too high above another.

Swedes and their egalitarian bent had to be responsible for this
sameness in the graveyard. They've carried their group mentality
too far, I thought.

I started to embroider what I wanted to know about the
deceased: Axel Andersson, 1888–1973, *Caught a Record Twenty-*
Five-Pound Pike/Was Nice to Children. Hanna Johansson, 1920–
1968, *Schoolteacher, Mother, Wife, Wrote Poetry.* Elsa Magnusson
1925–1985, *Gossip.* Hugo Carlsson, 1904–1960, *Pain in the Neck.*

I walked along the gravel path, examining the headstones.
Gold lettering on some of the gravestones made them look
bright and new. On others, etched crosses, flowers, haloed
figures, and fleur-de-lis decorated the names. Other stones,
worn by wind and rain, hosted patches of lichen, obscuring
the names of the deceased. One of my favorite grave markers
was that belonging to a certain Torsten Petersson. It consisted
of a cross made from sticks held together with a brass plaque
bearing the name and date. Either his family hadn't bothered
with the expense of a headstone or he had no family. There
was no way of knowing.

Familjegravarna (family graves), with an engraved list of
the individuals stacked under the headstone, caused me to
wonder. Which family do you bury yourself with: the one
you were born in or the one you married into? What if you
didn't like your in-laws and had to spend eternity stretched
out next to them? Then there were the logistics of opening
the grave and rearranging coffins so that everyone who
wanted in could get in. I noticed a fresh grave site. The coffin,
marked by the dirt that covered it, was turned sideways, per-
pendicular to the headstone.

Something else caught my eye. Surviving spouses were
listed with their birth dates and a dash, leaving a blank space

to be filled in upon their demise. What if you remarried? What would it be like to see your name on a tombstone? I guess Ebenezer Scrooge knew.

The midafternoon light filtered through the birch trees, making the atmosphere in the cemetery calm and serene. In the distance, a woman in gloves snipped and pruned the foliage. We approached her, for we hadn't had any luck finding Kurt's grave. She was a trim, attractive woman with a bright face. I had not expected to find someone so cheerful working in a cemetery. The woman tossed aside some old branches, wiped her forehead with the back of her hand, and told us that the registration of grave sites was located in the pastor's office, but that unfortunately the office was closed. If it was a recent death, she explained, he might be to the northern or western ends of the cemetery, which was where the newer grave sites were being dug. Had he been cremated, he would be up near the meditation gardens. She pointed behind her, and we could see small markers laid out on the side of a small hill. We thanked her. She returned to the task of trimming a hedge.

Eva walked slowly, glancing around her as she went. Lars moved more quickly; he didn't seem interested in studying names he did not recognize. He wanted to help his mother find what she was looking for. I searched one side of the grounds and was absorbed in reading names, making up identities for the deceased, and studying the layout of stones and old markers. When I found Kurt's gravestone, I felt as if I had found an egg at Easter. Lars and Eva were nowhere in sight. I called their names.

"We're over here!" hollered Lars from behind a dense shrub on the other side of the church.

I went over and found Eva looking down at an old headstone. The names had been eroded completely. You couldn't read them even when you traced what was left of the letters with your finger.

"This is where my mother is buried, my father, and my grandmother," Eva said to me in English, then bent over to clear away dead leaves. Lars had gotten a small spade from the workstation and began digging up weeds, clearing a place to put the flowers. Eva suddenly looked small. Her arms hung weakly at her sides. Seventy-four years old and the grief of losing her parents remained so near the surface. This was the moment I had feared. I moved closer to her. She pointed to a large white marble headstone with gilded lettering.

"That is the grave of my uncle and aunt, the people who raised me."

Eva's childhood story is a hard one to relate, because in the telling great sadness gets exposed, and people get blamed—the people that Eva tried to love and wanted to be loved by. Eva's father had died of pneumonia, leaving behind a young wife and two small daughters. They quickly became destitute. The meager income her mother earned as a seamstress could provide for at least one of her children, but there was not enough money to buy food for both of them. The authorities forced her to give one of her children away. It is not known how it was decided which daughter to give away, but Eva's uncle (her father's brother) and his wife took Eva in to live with them and their children. Eva saw her mother and older sister now and then, but she was not even allowed overnight visits, weekends, or holidays. The oddest thing about this arrangement was that the aunt and uncle lived less than a block away from Eva's mother, yet on several occasions when Eva begged to see her mother, her aunt and uncle had locked her in a closet, so that no one could hear her calling and crying.

Eva has said that her aunt and uncle were kind to her, but she has also told stories about being abused. She was hurt and angry and grateful all at the same time.

"If the aunt and uncle had enough money to take care of Eva, why didn't they just give food or extra money to the mother, so Eva could stay with her family?" I once asked Lars.

Lars didn't know why.

At family gatherings Eva will sometimes take us back to that childhood closet, back into the darkness in which she cried and nobody came. We tap our fingers against the rims of our wineglasses and look up at the ceiling, at the clock, or down at our plates. She will say, "My poor mother. My poor mother had such a hard life."

She will never say: "I hate her, and I hate them, and I hate everyone for dying and leaving me."

Someone will touch her shoulder. Someone else will try to change the subject. She will cry and ask, "Why? *Why?*"

Eva gave her uncle's *familjegrav* a sideways glance. He had been a successful local politician, and after he died his friends erected this tombstone in honor of him and his family. The small gray postage stamp of a grave marker belonging to Eva's *familjegrav* was, I am told, a recycled tombstone.

"How do you get a recycled tombstone? Wasn't somebody using it?" I whispered to Lars.

He had heard that old graves were sometimes dug up to

make room for new ones. The bones of the forgotten deceased were put into a communal grave, and the old headstones were offered cheap.

I stared at the disparity between the white marble stone with gold lettering and the dull gray stone. I wanted to hold Eva and tell her, "These are just rocks. Don't mind them. They don't mean anything." Instead I just stared and wished I did not see what I could see.

Lars arranged the cut flowers in the vase and placed it next to his grandparents' headstone. He turned and spoke to his mother, and she responded by leaning over and centering the vase. I announced that I had found Kurt. I pointed and they followed me across the churchyard.

Eva had saved a few flowers for Kurt. While she arranged them before his simple granite headstone, the silence was filled by the clipping of the groundskeeper's shears in the distance and the *she-wish, she-wish, she-wish* of a water sprinkler. The sun in the western sky filtered through the tree branches. Lars crumpled the pink florist paper into a ball, and together we walked back to the car.

The church and graveyard grew smaller and smaller behind us as we followed the road down the hill and across the bridge. I thought about the fisherman who had caught that record salmon so many years before. Those days are gone now. What remains behind are memories of childhood, love, a record catch, and enough grief to last a lifetime. Like the river flowing beneath us, life shines briefly in the fading light, then disappears around the bend.

Fishing the Threshold

IDSJÖSTRÖMMEN WAS ONLY a five-minute drive from the house. This was the closest I had ever lived to water, but I still didn't seem to be saving any time getting ready to fish. I kept promising myself *to get more organized,* so that I might get dressed, put the rod together, and head toward the river, ready to fish, all in one fluid movement. But this never seemed to happen. Tinkering with fishing gear was as much a part of going fishing as fishing, and I have tried to accept this, yet regardless of how well I have prepared, I always seem to be thirty minutes away from the first cast.

What happens is that I can't find my wading socks. Searching for my socks takes at least twenty minutes. Maybe I find my wading socks and arrive streamside with all my gear only to discover that my leader needs to be lengthened. While I lengthen the leader by tying on sections of tippet material, I see that I am out of 4X tippet material, and look in my vest for that new spool that I am sure I put in a pocket last time I went fishing—or would that have been in some other vest? While I'm looking for the tippet, my fly box drops and breaks open on the ground at my feet. The wind is blowing, and the flies bounce out of the box and skitter across the parking area.

Like a pilot, I have to work through a checklist before taking off. I must always carefully look through vest pockets, inspect leader for wind knots, change tippets, examine fly boxes, put loose split-shot back in the little container they always fall out of, make sure I have my polarized glasses, and string my rod. Then I can go.

One day in the middle of July I went to fish Idsjöströmmen in an area I call the Threshold. The Threshold lies in the river's upper section, and consists of a wall of stones that extend into the middle of the river. The current tumbles over it, then drops and churns into a white froth that eventually plays itself out. While I pulled on waders and wading boots, I thought about the fish holding beneath the Threshold, on the downstream side, where a three-ton boulder sits, battered by the current. This boulder is fitted with an old rusty iron ring about the size of a man's hand, a leftover from the logging days when it served to secure guidelines. There are grayling that prefer the deep pool near this boulder, where they hide under cover of turbulent water, waiting for food to float by. I envisioned the Gim River dry flies and nymphs that Lars had tied for me mixing in with the "naturals" and being taken by one of these determined grayling.

After thirty minutes of fumbling with tippet spools, searching pockets for the dry-fly box, finding it, picking out nymphs that had gotten into the dry-fly box, and putting them into the nymph box, which somehow had been moved to another pocket, I was finally ready. I locked the car, shuffled down the embankment, and stepped into the river. I found my way downstream, and along the way cast to several pools with Lars's Gim River Fluttering Stone, a dry fly. A few small grayling went for it. Pleased with that promising start, I pressed onward.

The river roared over the Threshold, drowning out all other sounds. Fly-fishing books with chapters titled "Safety When Wading," or "What Not to Do When Fishing" will tell you not to stand on large rocks in rivers—especially in rough water. Stepping back into the water isn't as easy as climbing out. You can expect to get knocked off your feet, causing you to lose your rod, your hat, and anything in open vest pockets. It will all float downstream while you struggle to reach land.

With each step I took, the river current pushed hard on my legs, threatening to bowl me over. Breaking the rules, I pitched myself up onto the heights of the Threshold. Wedging my feet securely between the rocks and jamming my wading staff tight into a rock crevice where I could easily reach it, I was free to use both hands to cast and retrieve line.

My cast was neither beautiful nor fine; it was an attack. I tossed the line up into the air and slammed it down forcefully into the current. This approach pushed the weighted nymph into the rushing water, so that it sank faster to the river bottom, where the fish were. The current pulled and drew the line away. I swung the rod tip in front of me, causing the nymph to look as if it were swimming. This inspired a solid hit. I set the hook.

In some fly-fishing book on a dusty shelf somewhere in my office is a sentence that reads, "You should take care to study the river. Know where you are going to fish and how to get back before you get yourself into a dangerous or life-threatening situation." But trouble doesn't always present itself up-front; neither does success. I hadn't thought much past *trying* to catch a fish. In my hurry to get up on the Threshold I had forgotten to look ahead and see where I would need to go with a grayling heaving and pulsing on the line. Pulling the fish up through the powerful current meant possibly harming it, or losing it altogether. To net the grayling, I would need to get downstream by slipping through an opening in the stone wall near the left bank.

Holding the rod—heavily bent by the grayling—in one hand, I took hold of my wading staff in the other and shakily stepped off the Threshold. Passing through that opening, I had to keep left in order to stay in wadable water, and yet at the same time avoid being snagged by the drooping willow and birch branches from the trees growing close to the river. Experience had already taught me that if I stepped too far to the right, the cold river would breach the top of my chest waders, soak my sweater, then, while I gasped, trickle all the way down into my socks. But I made the move without difficulty and waded to a back eddy. There I brought the grayling in.

Things went well—not exactly by the fishing book, but

good enough. I seemed to have met all the challenges that had presented themselves. Suddenly I became aware of the scene around me: the sweet smell of a birch-wood campfire some fishermen had started across the river, the lushness of the green fir forest crowding each side of the river, the sight of swifts diving through the air. I experienced a kind of joy, a glorious stillness of the heart. On my line I had a healthy one-pound grayling flashing its deep burgundy-red–trimmed dorsal fin when it surfaced, and a beautiful river to play it in. I was completely satisfied. *How rare,* I thought.

Then my rod tip snapped.

I'm certain I have read in some fishing book that it is a good idea to bring along an extra rod in case something happens to the one in use. Or maybe it said, "You should own more than one rod and travel with them at all times," or, "Always bring a friend along who has rods to loan." Whatever the case, I hadn't followed the advice.

To bring the grayling to hand, I had raised my arm and backed it into a tangle of birch tree branches above me, thus breaking the fragile tip. I had to respond quickly for the sake of my stranded catch. I tossed the rod, reel first, back into the brush and took hold of the fly line. I could feel the grayling shaking its head. The fish had been so patient. I was the one who had gotten us into this mess, and I had to be the one to get us out.

I grabbed the line and, hand over hand, carefully pulled the grayling in. The barbless hook slipped out easily as I backed it away from the grayling's upper lip. Tossing the leader and line aside, I made my usual effort to revive the fish by supporting it, nose-first, upstream in the water. The grayling rested calmly in my hands until it was ready to slip back into the stream.

I looked back at the Threshold and figured it would take about twenty minutes to wade out, drive home, pick up another rod, and be back in the water—actually, it was more like fifty.

Walking the Forest

LARS INTRODUCED ME TO the forest trails by insisting I join him on a jog. A lifelong athlete, soccer player, cross-country ski instructor, and general exercise enthusiast, Lars can be very persuasive.

"Jog and walk," he said. "You need to exercise your heart muscle. We'll take it easy."

Exercising is not entirely foreign to me, but the older I get, the more excuses I find I can make to avoid it. For starters, I have weak ankles from ligaments torn playing sports, and I have asthma. This means I require a certain amount of

preparation before I can follow Lars on one of his training sessions. I have to lash on specially prescribed ankle supports and take two puffs on an inhaler.

So the idea of jogging on a forest trail terrified me as much as it intrigued me. All that uneven ground to roll ankles, and having to be constantly on the alert for tree roots, rocks, and sticks. I pranced after Lars, sure that at any moment my untrustworthy ankles would buckle and toss me facedown into the soft undergrowth.

I watched in amazement as Lars bounced along and then disappeared down the trail with the sprightliness of a deer. He reminded me of the athletes who train for the Olympics by running barefoot in the forests and jungles of their homeland. People from places without shopping malls to shield their citizens from the elements seem to be a lot tougher. I breathed heavily, tripped over an irregularity in the path, recovered, and pressed on cautiously.

Lars noticed that I was not directly behind him. He jogged back to me, then jogged in a circle around me and suggested I walk awhile. This spurred my competitive instinct and my shame at not being able to keep up with a man seventeen years older than I. I did the only thing a determined woman approaching forty could do. I said I would run when and how I damn well pleased and he could just go and ... Lars couldn't understand what I was saying because I needed huge drags of breath between each word, but he understood enough to know that things were heading south. Having been a schoolteacher for twenty years, he knew when to employ a distraction.

"Just down this way is a secret place," he said, heading off.

Wanting to forget my humiliation, I followed. We turned

off the main path and jogged down one less worn for about a hundred yards to a place deep in the woods. Tucked into the base of a small depression, near the foot of a large tree, was a spring that bubbled up from beneath the forest floor into a shallow pool. The water percolated up through fine sand, causing it to erupt in miniature bursts. We drank handfuls of the chilled pure water and wiped our faces with our sleeves. We listened to the trees creaking as they swayed and their branches rustled in a breeze.

In an old version of the Little Red Riding Hood story that I used to read as a child, the drawings placed the little girl, who in the drawings resembled a Hummel figure, in a fir forest. Pink wildflowers and slate-colored mushrooms grew along the pathway. A stone fence guarded her grandmother's red cottage. This secret place could easily have served as the model. I had often thought of that charming book, never believing that one day I would step into its pages.

Lars and I jogged and walked through the forest on several more occasions. Soon I was able to follow the unmarked paths on my own. Private treks into these woods became my daily ritual.

These treks offered me much to conjure with. In one place, anthills the size of washing machines seemed to grow out of the base of tree trunks. I counted over twenty-five of them. Each hill teemed with thousands of busy red ants. I discovered that the call of the cuckoo really is onomatopoeic for the bird's name. I listened to woodpeckers machine-gunning holes in the trees and wondered what cumulative effects so much knocking would have on their heads. Warblers twittered and trilled their songs in distinctive patterns as the males marked their territory and beckoned the females. In this festive atmosphere I could forget my worries, that never-ending list of things to do. I found myself whistling back to the birds and deeply inhaling the balsam-scented air.

The particular route I liked best took about an hour to complete. It wound down behind our house toward a nearby lake, along the length of the lake, up over a steep hill, and then through several backyards until it reached our house again. During my walks I never saw another person, but I knew I had not been the only one to venture into the woods. Sometimes there were fresh shoe prints and paw prints in the soft mud. Word that the blueberries had begun to ripen, and that lingonberries would be early, had begun to spread in the village.

One day I decided to take Peter with me. He was eager to tag along. A chatty, communicative child, he walked along next to me and carried on with his usual enthusiasm for conversation. He talked and talked and talked, until even the sound of the birds was drowned out.

"Peter, when we are on a walk, it's important to me that we not talk too much. Listen to the trees, look around, notice where you are. We can't talk all the time."

Within five minutes he was at it again.

"Peter, I'll give you a krona if you stop talking for at least fifteen minutes."

Five minutes later he wanted to know if fifteen minutes were up. Remembering Lars's schoolteacher approach, I looked for a distraction. We came upon an anthill.

"Here, Peter, I've got bread crumbs. Take the bread and crumble it over the ants. See how they attack it?"

One ant grabbed a piece of bread three times larger than itself and began trying to haul it away. Three other ants came over to assist. They tickled each other with their little antennae—ant sign language, I supposed—then coordinated their efforts and together started toting the booty home.

"Hey, guys, look at all this free food from heaven!" said Peter as he shook more bread over the hill. The ants swarmed over the crumbs.

Showering them with bread amused us for a while. Staring at creatures the size of a pencil tip and seeing that they had organization and communication skills, in addition to admirable work habits, made me wonder what really went on in their tiny little brains. Perhaps they were highly evolved. Scary to think that the smaller you got, the more complicated you might be.

Speaking of small creatures, although the night before we left for Sweden I had told Peter that trolls did not exist, he still wanted to talk about them. In Swedish folklore, trolls look like miniature humans with pointed ears and long tails. They live in forests and in caves. Some are not particularly friendly. Traditionally, Scandinavian children were told stories about trolls, just as children in America are told about Little Red Riding Hood. Some of the stories about less friendly trolls were meant to warn children about the dangers of carelessly wandering alone in the forest.

"Do they come after people? What would they do to you if you met one?" asked Peter.

It certainly seemed plausible that something very much like a troll might exist in a Swedish forest, but not wanting my son's imagination to run away with him, I felt I had to remind him that they did not exist. "Trolls are just made up by people who like to tell stories," I said.

"Do you promise?"

"I promise you, Peter. There are no such things as trolls."

We came to the part of the path that turned and followed the backyard perimeters of several village houses. As we approached the first lot, I could see the bony figure of a little old man stooping to rake cuttings and carry them to a compost heap. A troll? I wondered. When the old fellow saw us he froze. We had to pass directly in front of him to continue along the path. I smiled and said, "Hello! How are you." Leaning on the rake for support, he turned away, like a child refusing a spoonful of food. I smiled and we walked on.

"Mom, why didn't that man say anything?"

"I think we surprised him."

The walk over, Peter went to see if one of the neighbor boys wanted to play. I went into the house. Lars was in his office.

"Who is the elderly man near the middle of the village? I think we frightened him."

"He's just one of the retired villagers," said Lars.

The next day I took my forest walk alone. As I came up to the old man's yard I felt a little uncomfortable. I didn't want to bother him again, but I had to go through his property to stay on the trail.

The area behind his house was immaculate. The lawn was clipped neatly and evenly. A *gärdesgård* (rustic wooden fence) enclosed a stand of the tallest, straightest pine trees I had ever seen. They were at least three stories high and evenly spaced. Then I noticed a piece of paper tacked to a tree trunk, facing the path. It hadn't been there the day before. There was writing on it. I stepped closer to have a look. It was in Swedish.

Lars agreed to go with me on my next walk in the forest to translate. The paper was still there fluttering in the breeze.

"It says, Don't Touch My Trees."

"Why do you think it says that?"

"He used to have more forest, but he sold it. I think this is all he has left. He's protecting it."

As I stood there I thought how things must be for the old man. Don't Touch My Trees seemed a desperate message. I understood a little how he felt. Life can be frightening at times, whether because of uneven ground, wolves, trolls, or strangers emerging unexpectedly from the dark forest babbling in a foreign tongue. It's enough to inspire anyone to post a warning. Still, there were also bubbling springs, birdsongs, and crumbs from heaven, but before we walked away, I reached out and patted one of the old man's trees.

The Biting Season

ON MY DAILY WALK in the forest I occasionally met up with Bengt, who would be out exercising his hunting dog. We would begin our conversation with observations about the weather and the impending mosquito season.

If I said, "It's cold," he would say, "Yes, but no mosquitoes." If I said, "It's windy," he would say, "Yes, but no mosquitoes." If I said, "Beautiful weather," he would say, "Mosquitoes, but they were worse last year." When it was dry he would say, "If it rains, next year, many mosquitoes." When it rained, he would say, "Many mosquitoes this year, very dry last year."

Bengt was a kind of all-the-mosquito-news-all-the-time station. But despite his interest in their arrival and their numbers, he didn't seem bothered about them when they did show up. In the outdoors, where other mere mortals fear to tread without ointment or veil, Bengt walked bare-armed and free at the height of mosquito season. He didn't flinch when a mosquito hovered in front of his face either.

"Don't you get tired of being bit?" I once asked him.

"Ah," he said, "I'm too old for them to bite anymore."

Swedish newscasts reported that during a bad mosquito year farm animals might actually die from the bites and from the stress of being bitten. I could almost see one of the black-and-white cows, so prevalent in the countryside, sink to its knees, roll onto its back, and expire with all four feet sticking into the air, while Bengt pointed to it and said, looking straight into the camera, "Many mosquitoes this year."

Some unlucky hikers and campers can suffer a kind of mosquito shock if they get caught in an infested area. The constant high-pitched whine of a billion mosquitoes and the bites create a crisis, both mental and physical. On one particular fishing trip to the Swedish mountains, Lars said that he sprinted from the river as fast as he could, slapping his legs and rubbing his arms to rid his clothing of mosquitoes. Then he dove into his tent and frantically zippered the flap shut behind him. Inside, he listened to the mosquitoes trying to get in through the tent's roofing and siding. He said it sounded like rain.

In the forest country we also had *småsven* (literally, "small

Svens"). I am not an entomologist, but I would say that they were the same critter as a no-see-um. This microscopic insect has a bite one thousand times its size. When you walk on the lawn in the coolness of a summer evening, they pop up from the ground and latch onto your legs like fleas. And if you don't walk across the lawn, they fly around looking for you anyway. Picnicking diners have to dash into the house with plates and covered dishes when the *småsven* arrive.

You know a *småsven* has bitten you when it feels as if someone has just yanked a hair out of your arm. If somehow you miss the bite, you'll recognize the hit by the itchy red bump that soon follows.

Then there are the ants. They're red like a warning. If you carelessly sit or lie on the ground near one of their colonies, they will eventually crawl onto exposed flesh, then go to work with their little jaws. Sometimes you feel the bite, sometimes you don't, but you're left with red marks that can last for weeks. And there's no escape. They're everywhere. After walks in the forest I have found them teething on my ankles, feet, and toes. I have found them on the ground where I sit and eat my lunch. I have found them on the sand where I had laid my beach towel. When I look very closely at the forest floor, there are so many ants it looks like a living carpet. One must be willing to live dangerously.

If the ants, mosquitoes, or *småsven* don't get you, the *broms* will. *Broms,* which come out in mid-July, have delta-shaped wings and green eyes and are about the same size as a housefly. Their tactic is to provoke you by circling endlessly around your head. As soon as you start waving hands wildly about, trying to fend them off, several will attach themselves to the back of your neck or legs. Something about the way they bite makes them pain-free; you don't feel anything until they withdraw their bug-teeth. Then you experience a terrible stinging and see blood trickling out of the wound. The one good thing about *broms* is that they are none too quick. Their wings wrinkle like tissue paper when you bat them off your arm or leg. If you stay calm, you can easily swat them dead before they do any damage.

Honeybees, bumblebees, and wasps exist in Sweden as well, but they are not programmed to search and attack. There are horseflies too, but they are obvious and are easily brushed away.

July is the high season for biting bugs. Walks in the forest are therefore best enjoyed at a jog. If you dare to stop and listen, you can hear the whine of billions and billions of mosquitoes. Just the sound makes you itch all over. Experienced outdoor enthusiasts know that smoke from a campfire helps drive flying, biting bugs away. Swedes cut themselves a switch of green birch branches and rhythmically wave it about their heads and shoulders. If they must, they might break down and apply repellent. Fishers have discovered that retreating to the river is the best option. A slight breeze is almost always blowing over the water and the mosquitoes there don't seem to be half as bad.

But I soon learned that true Swedish forest people mustn't look bothered by biting insects, especially mosquitoes. No squealing, swearing, or sudden jerky movements to indicate something has bitten or is about to bite. No preapplication of repellent in the house, car, or parking area. Mosquitoes must be sighted and proved to be an actual nuisance. Even then, repellent is applied inconspicuously, if at all. You must never use hats veiled with netting, beds draped with netting, special sonic devices, vitamin preparations, or lemon-scented candles to drive mosquitoes away. Locals view dependence on any of these items as indicating weakness of character. Only foreigners, or people from Stockholm, use any of the above.

Warning: Do not swat someone else's mosquito. Mind your own business. People are responsible for their own bites. In-house mosquito executions are acceptable, but you must not swat when they land on the wall, especially on wallpaper. The stains left by squashed blood-engorged mosquito bodies are nearly impossible to remove. You must learn to snatch a pesky mosquito out of the air with your bare hand, then hold it in your fist as if rolling dice. Finally, bring your hand down on your thigh, opening the palm at the last possible second. Inspect hand and thigh for bug parts to confirm kill. For quicker results, simply clap your hands together, then nonchalantly open them and let the offensive creature float gently to its final place of rest.

When someone has left a window or door open, or forgotten to close the chimney flu, fighting back becomes a real challenge; you can't clap or swat fast enough. That's when you bring out the trusty Volta—the vacuum—whose long hose and pipe attachments allow one to chase after any winged creature that has entered domestic airspace and suck it into the dusty darkness of the vacuum bag.

Once, Lars and I had a plague of over one hundred mosquitoes in the kitchen. More were in our sleeping area. Still more roamed the hall. Lars thought they had snuck in when the front door was left open, but I was convinced they had come in through the cracks of the unfinished second floor. During a particularly bad night, the high-pitched whine of mosquitoes looking for skin nearly drove us insane. What little sleep we got left us with red itching marks on our foreheads and arms.

The next day I brought out the Volta. Motor blasting, I hoisted up the silver tube and pointed it at every mosquito in sight. I enjoyed doing this.

Then arrives that day, sometime around mid-August, when little insect legs and wings quit tickling your arms. It has grown strangely silent. It is safe to leave the windows and doors open. Nothing comes after you looking for a vein. Once the season of biting is over, Swedes are very forgiving. They tend to forget what they have recently endured. It is enough that the mosquitoes have left, and won't be back for another year. Until then, no one wants to talk about them. Not even Bengt.

The Man on the Bridge
and the Naked Lady

AS THE SUMMER PROGRESSED, more and more fly fishers, mostly men, either alone or with a buddy or in a small group, arrived to fish the grayling waters of Idsjöströmmen. They had come from places far away, sometimes driving all night. They stepped from their cars, sporting road-weary grins and soft-brimmed hats rumpled from weather and long use. Eager and ready, they hurriedly checked into Kullagården, or set up their tents along the riverbank. Within an hour they had tugged on waders, donned fishing vests, strung their rods, and advanced with staccato steps toward the river.

Only then, with the reverence of pilgrims, did these fly fishers pause, allowing the sights and sounds of Idsjöströmmen to wash over them like baptismal water. Soon they had plotted where to fish, moved in that direction, and, as if easing into a nice warm bath, stepped into the current.

On a bright July day late in the afternoon I joined them, arriving just before another fly fisher driving a silver Volvo careered dangerously into the parking area and came to a stop. The driver extracted himself from the car, then slammed the door like an exclamation mark. This was clearly his first day off work. He was wearing green fatigues, a red plaid flannel shirt, and the requisite rumpled fishing hat. Muttering to himself, he opened the trunk, lifted out tackle bags and rod tubes, placed them on the ground, then immersed his arms, elbow-deep, in their contents.

Avoiding conversation, I walked to the first windbreak just beyond the parking area. There I sat down on a tree stump and put on my waders. The mosquitoes were particularly fierce; I made an extra effort to ignore them while tying the laces of my wading boots. Finally, wearing waders and vest, and with fly rod ready, I stood up. I noticed that the man had finished his preparations and walked up onto the bridge that marks the upper boundary of the river. He paced and circled, then, his left hand raised, palm inward, stopped. With his right hand he punched the buttons of a cell phone, put it to his ear, and, to my horror, started shouting into it.

It seemed to me that if a man had an entire bridge on which to shout anything, it should be "I LOVE HER," or "I WANT HER TO BE THE MOTHER OF MY CHILDREN." Something like that. But no—this man was accusing someone of having "INSUFFICIENT FUNDS on an

OVERDRAWN ACCOUNT." Fishers on both sides of the river looked up from under the brims of their hats.

Disgusted, I turned and marched toward the trail leading to the lower section of the river. The trail was bordered with brilliant green ferns, and blueberry shrub flourishing under a canopy of fir and birch. Come fall, mushrooms would pop up in the shadows overnight. After a few hundred yards the trail opened into a place where the trees had been thinned by a timber sale. The sun warmed my back while I continued toward what we called the Alligator Swamp—where springs near the ground's surface have turned the trail and surrounding area into a muddy mess. This is a place where boots have been sucked off their owners' feet, mosquitoes breed with abandon, and it doesn't smell so great, especially on a hot day. I cleared Alligator Swamp, swatting mosquitoes as I stumbled along.

Soon I had arrived at the second windbreak. Draped over the branches of a nearby birch tree, a pair of wet socks and a shirt hung drying. Inside the windbreak sat Stig, an older gentleman, eating a ham sandwich. Jackets hung on pegs along the walls. Triangia stoves (lightweight Swedish-made camp stoves) sat on the benches, along with thermoses and coolers, indicating the presence of other fishermen in the area. Stig's brown neoprene waders were covered with rubbery-looking bumps, the result of repairing rips and snags with silicone glue. He had on a tan camouflage shirt and a weathered black felt hat banded with a brightly woven cloth. Stig never said much. He finished his sandwich and took out a pipe.

Four fly fishers were on the water before us. One was netting a good-sized grayling, which only minutes before had been down deep in one of the many pools found in this part of the river. We celebrated his success with a round of applause.

"Any fishing upstream?" Stig asked.

"Yes, earlier this morning when Lars and I checked the river they were rising to elk hair caddis."

Stig nodded in acknowledgment before knocking the ashes from his pipe by tapping it on the bottom of his boot. Next he pulled a pouch of tobacco from his shirt pocket, tamped some into the bowl, then held a lighter over it and drew hard, pulling the flames down into the tobacco. I enjoy the sweet and woodsy smell of a pipe. It also helps keep mosquitoes away. This made Stig the perfect person to sit with. We stared quietly at the river and the fishermen, while wisps of smoke hung above our heads like sketched thoughts.

Across the river from the second windbreak and a little downstream is another access called Strömsbaken ("the hill by the stream"). People often bring a trailer and park it there during their stay, which is exactly what one of our fly fishers and his girlfriend had done. I noticed her, a nonfisher in a bikini, as she flapped a towel and laid it on the grassy knoll overlooking the river. Lying on her stomach, she obviously intended to soak up some sun while admiring her fly-fishing boyfriend as he fished.

I turned my attention to a gentleman in front of us. His casts were smooth and beautiful. Just upstream, another fisher was having some success in a smaller pool, and downstream, yet another had waded out into deep water and was struggling against the current, intently drifting a weighted nymph. All were fishing as if it was a question that needed to be answered. If I could have painted that scene I would have made it abstract, just lines and paint hinting at the fact that there were people standing in a river fly fishing, because as much as they were there, they were not there.

Stig offered to make some coffee. I went in search of kindling while he filled the blackened resident coffeepot with fresh water. Together we engineered the stoking of the fire and the boiling. Making coffee next to a favorite river is part of the reason a person goes fishing in the first place. Coffee prepared over an open fire tastes better than any other, even when there are bugs, soot, or a little moss floating in the cup. Inconvenience is an accepted condition of being in the outdoors.

We sipped our flavorful dark coffee and quietly discussed what the afternoon's fishing might bring. Suddenly a scream, terrible and shrill, came from across the river.

I leaped to my feet. The girlfriend on the hill had shed her bikini to catch *all* the sun's rays and was now running back and forth naked, screaming in high C. Every fly fisher shifted his focus from his floating flies and strike indicators to her. She rubbed her short blond hair vigorously, as if trying to shampoo something out. She alternately slapped her thighs, slapped her arms, and galloped in the downstream direction, her bottom jiggling like two plates of *lutfisk*. Then she turned and loped back upstream, her ample breasts swaying like two Swedish flags in the wind. In a final frenzied flourish of shaking, waving, slapping, and screaming, she found her way to the trailer door, opened it, jumped inside, and slammed it shut. Her fly-fisher boyfriend studied the empty beach towel and the stone-silent trailer, then calmly began to reel in his line. Stig stood at my elbow. His pipe had gone out and hung loosely from the corner of his mouth.

"*Mygg*," he said.

Yes, the mosquitoes had been thick that day. The poor woman had obviously also discovered the ants. The fly fishers acknowledged the woman's dance of pain with a gentle chorus of chuckles. Then, with little smiles on their faces, they returned to their fishing.

It was time for Stig and me to join them. We waded into the waters of Idsjöströmmen to try and forget the man on the bridge and the naked lady. After all, whether it's an overdrawn account or a towel full of ants, there's always something to scream about. With each cast I was reminded that the focused distraction of fly fishing has kept more than one person sane, and helped heal their mosquito-bit souls before they journey back home.

Cigar Smoke and Split Cane

IN MID-JULY Lars and I fished Idsjöströmmen together. It was early one afternoon on a lower section of the river that I had not fished before. I had been fishing without a break for nearly three hours when I noticed a large boulder with an obvious flat spot to sit on, so I reeled up, waded over, and sat down. In my vest pocket was a cellophane-wrapped cigar. I had been puffing on cigars on windless days in July to keep the mosquitoes and *broms* away from my face.

My father smoked cigars when he was in a good mood, and because of that I've always liked the smell. When I was about fourteen my Uncle Ralph found it extremely amusing to let me smoke cigars. His invitation to smoke came after he and my dad had mixed a few martinis and were in a jovial mood. Uncle Ralph would get out his humidor, offer cigars all around, and insist I take one. I would take a short, narrow one from the cedar-lined box. Uncle Ralph would sit back and watch, then laugh and laugh at the sight of a teenage girl with two long braids and a lit cigar sticking out of her mouth. My aunt Joan walked in once and discovered us making idiots out of ourselves in a haze of cigar smoke. She shook her finger at Uncle Ralph.

"She shouldn't be doing that!"

He just smiled, and then taught me how to blow smoke rings. I adored my Uncle Ralph.

I unwrapped the cigar and lit it. While I smoked I directed my attention upstream, where Lars was thoroughly combing a run, setting the hook about every third cast. I never got jealous when he caught fish; I just liked to watch him at work—his precise and accurate presentations, his methods for fooling fish, his being possessed by the entire act.

I began amusing myself by trying to make those perfect rings of smoke Uncle Ralph had taught me. A good cigar tastes the way a good campfire feels—warm and welcoming. I took a drag, tilted my head back, made a tight circle out of my lips, and pushed the smoke from my mouth. About five out of ten could be recognized as smoke rings. One really good one floated up over my head. I grinned in delight.

Carl Larsson, the famous Swedish artist, painted his daughter Lisbeth standing on the dock at the family home in the village of Sundborn. She looks about eight years old in the picture. She is wearing a red tam, a blue plaid shirt, a solid blue skirt, and she is fishing. She is barefoot, and her back is to the viewer. She has tucked her rod, which is whittled from a tree branch, under her arm, while the rest of it hangs over the dock railing; the line dangles into the water below. I admire her uncomplicated approach. One does not need lots of gear to enjoy fishing—just the basic components of rod, line, and lure. This portrait of Lisbeth also reminds me of how important it is to keep pleasures simple.

Perhaps that's why I love the split-cane bamboo rod Lars gave me. It was custom-built by Swedish rod-maker Carl Anderberg and christened Squaw Creek Rod in honor of a day Lars and I had spent fishing a tributary by that name on the Gallatin River in Montana. The Squaw Creek Rod is seven-feet three-inches long and has two tips, burgundy wraps, and a rosewood reel seat. Traditionally, two tips come with a bamboo rod because after several days of fishing a bend or a set may occur in the tip. To prevent this, you must alternate your rod tip every other time you go fishing.

I like casting the Squaw Creek with a five-weight King Fisher silk line, which Lars also gave me. The line is spooled onto my Pflueger Progress reel, which once belonged to my great-grandfather. Bamboo quickly changed my fly-fishing life. I soon found it more and more difficult to feel any affection for graphite rods, though I had used them for years. I had become smitten with the six strips of durable grass reed, glued together and wrapped with colored threads, and there was no turning back.

The rod I cast that day on Idsjöströmmen was another split-cane rod called the Midsummer. It is a seven-foot nine-inch three-piece with a number five line, also built by Carl Anderberg. His signature burgundy wraps looked brilliant in the sunshine. I was as comfortable with this rod as I am with a favorite pair of shoes.

What I liked about the Midsummer was how easily it cast. It was light and responsive to quick changes in direction, yet long enough to mend the line decently on bigger water. Dry flies danced at the end of the leader, and when connected with a grayling, the Midsummer was forgiving yet steady in its response to the fish's resistance.

Split-cane rods feel more intimate than graphite rods, which are mass-produced. Graphite rods are light, strong, and designed to deal with any fishing situation. They come with lifetime guarantees. When your rod does for some reason break, you can ship the pieces back to the plant for repair. This is supposed to make spending hundreds of dollars for a stick more bearable.

Split-cane rods are handcrafted and take nearly one hundred hours to complete. They cost from several hundred to several thousand dollars depending on the quality and the reputation of the rod maker. Creating a cane rod involves splitting the bamboo, then cutting and hand-planing the cane strips to specific tapers and designs in order to create the kind of rod action desired (the split-cane rod builder deals in thousandths of an inch when it comes to the tapers). Next comes the gluing, the application of reel seat and reel seat hardware, ferrules, and guides. Many split-cane rod builders make their own ferrules (the stainless steel fittings at the end of the rod sections where the rod sections connect) and hardwood reel seat spacers. The finish must be chosen and applied with great skill so that the rod will survive its pending association with the elements. By the time a split-cane rod is completed, a lot of thought and care and time have been put into it.

I often think about the effort that went into the creation of my cane, and that is why I handle it with such care and respect. Unlike graphite and its open-ended relationship with its owner, a split-cane rod requires commitment. If I accidentally slammed it in a car door and snapped it in two, something deep inside of me would snap at the same time. My rod is unique—like the fish it will catch, and the day on which I catch it.

From my perch on top of the boulder I felt content simply to dangle my booted feet over the side as the river rolled on. Then, in a pool off to my right, like the first note of a song, a fish rose. I stubbed out my cigar, put it in my top left vest pocket, pushed off the boulder, slipped quietly back into the river, and cast. On the next rise the grayling I spied showed its magnificent dorsal fin as it took an egg-laying caddis. The obvious choice of fly was Lars's Gim River Fluttering Stone (which doubles nicely as an egg-laying caddis pattern). This Fluttering Stone is barely more than a hook with a blue-dun hackle mixed with a grizzly-hackle wound around it, looking more like a piece of laundry lint than an imitation of an egg-laying fly. But it rides high on the water, and when I twitch the rod tip ever so slightly I can make it look like a fly dipping its abdomen and delivering its eggs on the surface. My approach was to send the fly down to the fish from upstream. I found the current seam that lined up with the rising fish and dropped it in. My fly floated toward my target, like a spoon to a baby's mouth. The grayling took, I lifted the rod, and we discovered each other.

My Patch of Green

IN THE PLACES in the States where I have lived, parking lots are measured by how many football fields long and wide they are. Streets, freeways, housing developments, office complexes, and malls cover every inch, as far as the eye can see, making one's garden the only refuge from an increasingly man-made environment. Grass, flowers, and shade trees remind people that there is life beyond asphalt. Working in the yard, watering the plants, and mowing the lawn all help us reconnect to nature.

But as Lars's former father-in-law used to say (so Lars told me), "The forest should remain in the forest." With all the greenery and natural beauty that the Swedish countryside offers, a lawn doesn't serve the same purpose as it does in the American suburbs. Here, a lawn is the zone between you and a hungry forest. If you don't mark off your space before the summer is fully under way, the growth will become so thick you won't be able to cut it back without specialized forestry equipment. Birch trees, wild grasses, and stinging nettles will help themselves to any untended plot of ground and, putting roots down and pushing leaves up, take hold. The next thing you know, after a good rain and dose after dose of twenty-four-hour sunlight, the forest will have crawled up the front porch into the house and strangled you in your sleep. In other words, mowing the lawn is a matter of survival.

There were two dented and rusted lawn mowers parked in a corner of the barn. At some point one had been cannibalized to repair the other, though upon close inspection it became clear both were out of order. And so it was off to Järn & Färg, the hardware store in Bräcke.

I love going to the hardware store. In the do-it-yourself world to which the Swedes (think of Ikea furniture) seem morally dedicated, the hardware store thrives. It is one of the only remaining businesses in the rural areas with a pulse. Along with the grocery store, the post office, the bank, the appliance shop, and the pizza place on the corner, the Järn & Färg in Bräcke has weathered bad times. There you will find what you need, and what you can't find, you don't need.

If I say Järn & Färg really fast it sounds like "yawn and fart," which, I discovered, was enough to send the six-year-old in the backseat into fits of hysterical laughter. This encouraged his mother to say it again and again, until the only real adult in the car asked both of us to please find another way to amuse ourselves. Phonetically, the correct pronunciation is "yearn oak ferry," and the name means "hardware and paint," but that just didn't have the same ring as yawn and fart.

We stepped into the Bräcke hardware store for a lawn mower. We passed the seasonal offerings for spring cleanup and planting: shovels, rakes, hoses, wheelbarrow, watering cans, window boxes, and gardening gloves. Then, right before our eyes, appeared a selection of lawn mowers. The choices were not rows and rows of various models, such as you might see at, say, a Home Depot. As with many things in Sweden, you get two choices: *this one* or *that one*.

I had nearly become convinced that this was another reason Swedes are such a very stable people. Their sanity is not tested every five minutes by having to make excruciating choices. Just ordering a cup of coffee in America wears me out. What flavor, what style? Caffeinated or decaffeinated? Skim or whole milk? Short or tall cup? Single or double? To stay or to go? And lastly, do I want that extra sleeve of cardboard to protect my grip from the scalding BTUs. Limited choices are sane, even when it comes to lawn mowers.

And actually, the hardware store had four candidates. The first was electric, designed for a very small yard. The cord limited your range, though of course you could always purchase an extension cord. You had to be careful not to let someone squirt it with a hose while you were operating it. Mower number two was a traditional gas-and-oil type machine, had lots of power, and a big bag for the grass to blow into. Mower number three was nearly identical to number two except that, instead of a bag, it mulched the lawn by blasting the clippings back to Mother Earth. Mower number four looked like a small tractor. We didn't have either that much money or that much lawn.

While Lars got involved in a spirited discussion with the hardware man, Peter and I quietly slipped away to have a look around. We walked the aisles and discovered bins full of nails and screws next to enormous spools of chain, electrical wiring, and rope. There were shelves of hammers, drills, Husquevarna (Swedish chain saws), and cans of paint. Stacked in a corner were rolls of linoleum, samples of birch-wood flooring, and an assortment of welcome mats including one that, in English, actually read, OH SHIT, NOT YOU AGAIN. Paintbrushes and cleaning supplies, buckets and mops, pots and pans—these were in the household section. Tape measures, extension cords, scissors, and balls of twine were sold next to the more colorful and interesting paint-by-number kits and home-brewing supplies. Swedish flags and flag poles wrapped in plastic were stacked at the end of the aisle closest to the register. The air smelled of rubber, metal, and oil.

After meandering around the store and examining all the different departments, we heard Lars's voice at the cash register and voices exchanging thanks. I figured that we had a new lawn mower, and indeed we did. When I met Lars at the car, I was introduced to mower number five. I don't know why I hadn't seen it. It was a push mower, the kind with a blade that spins inside a cylindrical chamber, as seen in *Leave It to Beaver* reruns.

"What is that?" I asked.

"We have such a small lawn I decided we could get some exercise at the same time we are mowing," replied Lars, sounding thoroughly convinced. "Besides, the others were too expensive. This way we can also save money."

He cinched the trunk down over the protruding handle with string. I thought about the tangles of thick knee-high plants whose names I didn't even know that had sprung up around our house.

"Lars, this thing won't cut the jungle we have growing and—"

"First we'll use the scythe that's in the barn to take down the tall grass, and then we can finish it with this. It will be fine, darling. I *promise* you."

Watching Lars swing the scythe through the yard made me feel like singing an old Soviet anthem. Peter was very curious about how the scythe worked, so Lars let him whack a few feet of greenery with it. Then we were instructed to grab a rake and clean up the first cutting. The sun had warmed things up considerably, and our T-shirts stuck to us front and back. We filled the wheelbarrow several times and dumped the contents off the back of the property. North, south, east, and west, the land was scythed, raked, and cleared of encroaching forest. It was time to bring in model number five.

I had the honor of trying it first. I grasped the handles firmly and proceeded to push it across the yard. After mowing two fifteen-foot rows, I lost my appreciative audience. Peter wandered off to explore somewhere; Lars disappeared into the house. I continued, but the blade got stuck and I had to clear it of grass. I hit the top of a hidden rock and had to maneuver the mower up and over. The blade got stuck again, and then again, as it choked on weeds and stems. To cut the grass to lawn length I had to mow the spot in front of me at least twice before I could take a step forward and start working on the next strip. Thirty minutes went by. I had covered—by my precise and exasperated measurements—one-sixteenth of the area. I might finish by midnight. In the distance I heard the familiar buzz of a real lawn mower, the kind that made grass magically disappear.

"LARRRRRRSSSSS!"

The next day we were back at the Yawn & Fart. We purchased a lawn mower with "easy start" operation. This meant no fewer than ten rotator-cuff–tearing yanks on the pull string before the engine sputtered to a full roar. But once it got going, all was forgiven. I marched up and down our modest yard, ruthlessly slaying wildflowers, grasses, and the beginnings of trees. The green moat around our island of civilization was secure, and we could sleep more easily at night.

Picking Berries

IN LATE JULY, the berry pickers in Sweden go on full alert. Blueberries and raspberries ripen at about the same time, followed by the bright-red lingonberries. If it has been a particularly good spring, without either frost or extreme temperatures, berry pickers look for *hjortron,* or "cloud-berries." In berry terms, cloudberries are nearly worth their weight in gold, bringing almost ten dollars a pound. They thrive in a moist environment, near water or in marshland, but are not easy to find. In fact, you can spend hours stooped over, gazing at the ground, looking for the distinct golden cluster of berries, which are about the same size and shape as a raspberry. A ripe cloudberry comes away easily from its stem. I didn't know any of this when I was invited to go picking. What I did know was that cloudberries were incredibly delicious. There is simply no better dessert than warm cloudberries served over vanilla ice cream or a slice of warm goat cheese. To me, they taste like caramel. Some people don't like the seeds, which are small and numerous, but I figure you can ignore seeds when something tastes this good.

Rumors spread that it was going to be a good cloudberry year. Once, when invited in for a cup of coffee by the neighbors, I spied a dozen or so sealed jars of these gems on the kitchen counter, still warm from the stove. I admired and praised them, but Lars had told me earlier it was not polite to ask where they had been picked. While some pickers may be willing to reveal their secrets, others will purposely misguide you, and still others will only smile and change the subject. But if you remain calm, they might give you a jar of cloudberries to take home.

Because of the rule of *Allemansrätten*—roaming rights—people from other countries, such as Poland, come to Sweden to pick berries as well. Polish berry pickers can earn what amounts to a year's salary in one month. You know they have arrived when you see at least five people crammed into a car so small it looks as if it was bought at a circus clown supply store. The berry pickers spend all day combing the forests, and will return with pounds of berries, which they will sell to jam-making and fruit companies, roadside stands, grocery stores, or tourists. Every year the pickers are interviewed on radio and television, which will carry special reports and updates on the berry-picking season. No one is required to belong to a union or carry insurance or have a work permit. They pick, sell, and head home.

I wasn't interested in berry picking to make money. I wanted to go because I craved cloudberries, and I had never picked berries before. Bengt generously offered to take Lars and me with him to his great cloudberry hunting grounds. He came by the house one day and picked us up in his car. Fifteen minutes later, he pulled off the side of the road and got out, then presented us each with a small plastic bucket, the kind children take to the beach. It all felt very wholesome—three adults walking into the woods holding cute little red sand buckets. But this was serious business. We walked quietly, talked quietly, and stared at the ground, looking for that glimmer of gold. Then we heard mosquitoes.

Slap! Slap! Slap!

"Here, let me give you some repellent," said Lars.

I didn't know which was more irritating—the mosquitoes or Lars applying the mosquito repellent.

"Stand still," he said as he rubbed the lemon-scented liquid on my neck, the tips of my ears, cheeks, forehead, and hands. I smelled like a lemon soaked in turpentine. This preparation appeared to confuse the mosquitoes. They hovered over my exposed skin, landed, lifted off, landed again, lifted off, landed, hovered, and whined. Mosquitoes are a nuisance whether or not they bite.

After twenty minutes of walking, Bengt finally picked a berry. I watched Lars stoop to pick one too. *We must be getting into some cloudberries,* I thought. I looked down and saw red berries with a touch of gold. I wasn't completely sure they actually were cloudberries, which I had only seen on postcards or after the real thing had been boiled and canned and all mashed up. *Maybe you can pick them a little on the red side and they ripen later.* Anyway, this was my first sighting of the berry, so in it went, *kerplunk* into the bucket. *Kerplunk,* another one, *kerplunk,* another. After I had found about ten, I noticed that there were more of them farther ahead. I walked to the next cluster of reddish-gold berries and *kerplunk* by *kerplunk* they went into the bucket.

Lars came over to see how I was progressing. His bucket was a quarter filled with golden cloudberries. He examined my collection and shook his head.

"Throw those out. They aren't ripe yet."

This meant I had to start all over again. With a sigh I poured what I had picked onto the ground.

"The berries are golden. Like this," he said, showing me what he had in his bucket.

The sun was out. It grew hot. We emerged from the trees that bordered the marshland, hunting and picking. Sometimes we found two or three in one place, sometimes more; there were areas where there were none at all. We had been picking for about an hour and had walked about a mile and our buckets were not even half full. We crossed an open area and began searching at the edges of the forest for signs of gold.

Slap. Slap. Kerplunk. Kerplunk. Slap. Kerplunk.

We didn't have any water. Lars unbuttoned his shirt and rolled up his sleeves. Bengt, wearing a T-shirt and jeans, walked and picked. He didn't talk. He didn't swat at mosquitoes either.

Two hours later, our buckets were still less than half full. It was humid. There was no breeze. We crossed another marsh. Bengt and Lars trotted along as if someone else might get to the berries before we did. I tried to keep up. Walking in a marsh is like slogging through sand. The soft ground forces you to lift your feet high and push off. You choose your next step carefully, lift high, and push off. I was wearing jeans, knee-high rubber boots, and a long-sleeved black sweater. My jeans were sweat-stuck to my legs. My black cotton sweater hung on me like wet laundry. I couldn't take any clothes off because of the mosquitoes. I felt like screaming, thinking it just might be the beginning of a nervous breakdown.

Bengt and Lars continued to stoop and pick. I felt faint. I found a patch of berries so thick I just sat down and picked my way through them. My pants got wet from the marshy ground. I didn't care. The mosquitoes surrounded me, relentlessly whining, and bit me through my clothes. I was determined not to complain. *Every Swede in the village did this,* I told myself. *Grandmothers could do this. I wanted to be thought of as one of them,* so I kept picking. *There will be jars of cloudberries on our kitchen counter as well,* I told myself. *Lars and I will give each other sly winks and not reveal our secret place but generously hand a jar to appreciative visitors. I'll decorate the lid with a blue-checked cloth and tie a ribbon around the top to secure it. Village women will smile and say, "Oh, I see you've been berry picking." We will all have something in common then. I'll show them. They'll see I'm making an effort.*

Three hours later, I was tired and hungry and miserable and wanted to say that maybe it was time to go back to the car, but I didn't trust myself to talk. If I opened my mouth, I would say, "Please, I can't do this anymore. I want to get out of here. I don't give a shit about cloudberry picking." I waited until Bengt asked if we wanted to leave.

On the long hot walk back to the car, we stopped by a

moose stand, a place where a hunter positions himself and quietly waits for a moose to come crashing through the brush so that he can shoot it. I decided I should try it sometime. It sounded easier than cloudberry picking.

Finally we reached the car and Bengt took us home. Before we went into our house, he generously emptied his berries into our buckets, giving us enough for about two jars. We thanked him for the afternoon and for giving us his share. He was pleased and waved in the rearview mirror as he drove away.

That night I warmed a cup of cloudberries in a saucepan. It took only a minute for the fruit clusters to break up and separate. The berry juice turned into warm bubbling syrup. I smelled the rich, unique scent and watched the steam rise. We toasted to our dessert of cloudberries over vanilla ice cream with small glasses of Swedish Punsch and then gave into it like a hungry kiss.

A few days later, I walked out to the main road to get the mail. Maud was working in her vegetable garden. Maud knew all the Swedish folk dances and practiced all the Swedish traditions. I thought she might be interested to know about my berry picking. We waved to each other and I crossed her lawn for a friendly chat. Eventually, I brought the conversation around to cloudberry picking.

"Oh! I *hate* cloudberry picking," said Maud.

"You do?"

"It's always so hot, and the berries are in—what you call in English—a bog?"

"Bog, marsh . . . right."

"And in the bog are many, many mosquitoes. Oh! It's so hot, hot, hot, and the mosquitoes . . . No! Never! I wait and get a jar from someone or buy it in the store. It's much better that way."

"You're right."

"Oh, and the mosquitoes!"

We nodded in agreement, our faces mirroring pained expressions.

Still, I was glad for the jar of cloudberries on our counter. But in the future if anyone noticed jars of cloudberries in our possession and, forgetting their manners, dared to ask where I had gotten them, I planned to smile and say, "Maud gave them to me."

Goat Farm

ANN KLENSMEDEN'S GOAT FARM is in Åsberet, a quiet hamlet in the forest about twelve miles from Gimdalen. The only sign indicating its location is posted just outside her farm, so unless you know where she lives, you probably won't find her; but ask anyone in the area and they will give directions. Lars and I stopped by several times during the summer to buy goat cheeses, jams, and the bread that her mother bakes.

Most of the buildings on the farm are well over a hundred years old. The barns and the original home were built with thick planks of timber, and are still painted traditional *falu röd*; the window frames are painted white. Flower boxes, thick with red, yellow, purple, and white petunias, hang from the front porch railing. Several ginger-colored chickens scratch and strut up and down the driveway and in and around the shrubbery. In a fenced meadow next to the house grazes a large gray Percheron mare straight from the pages of a Pippi Longstocking book. The horse moves lazily among ten or more recently weaned kid goats. On most summer days, the goat herd roams around the fenced pasture across the road from the farm. At milking time, when the goats are herded back into the barn, it's quite a parade.

A hired hand sometimes passes by in a large blue tractor on his way to the chicken barn, where Ann's father raises chickens for the poultry and egg market. One or more of Ann's three young children can usually be seen peering out the windows of the tractor's enclosed cab. Something about their unabashed gazes causes guests to stop and wave, then watch them until the tractor travels out of sight.

Almost immediately after visitors arrive, a medium-sized black mutt will greet them. He doesn't bite, but he does inspect newcomers with inquisitive sniffing and hand licking.

The farm is always busy. The sound of a loud discussion will rise above the roar of a motor; a hammer will begin banging; a door will slam. Visitors may feel they are intruding, and that maybe they should turn around and leave. However, if they just pet the dog and continue up the driveway toward the barn, eventually someone will emerge to meet them. Most often it is Maj, Ann Klensmeden's mother.

Ann's parents reside in the original farmhouse, across the yard from the newer home where Ann lives with her husband, Bo, and their children. Maj has graceful hands, kind, sweet, clear-blue eyes, a soothing voice, and she smiles all the time. I loved her from the minute I met her. She always greets Lars and me with a cheerful hello and walks us to their small cheese shop. If, for some reason, no one is at the shop, a note will be tacked to the door: HELP YOURSELF. PLEASE PUT THE MONEY IN THE REGISTER. THANK YOU.

But most of the time either Ann or her mother is there. Ann looks very much like her mother only more serious— serious enough so that when I first met her I have to admit that I felt intimidated. It wasn't because I thought she might be unpleasant, but because I sensed her dedication and discipline. Her life's work has been running her goat farm and making world-class gourmet cheeses. It is not a hobby; nor is it a back-to-nature exercise. When our eyes met for the first time I saw that she regarded me as a neophyte—not just new to Sweden but to life on a farm.

I was eager to get to know her, but fumbled with Swedish verbs and nouns like someone trying to find the right key to a locked door. Speaking in monosyllables with people at the grocery store or praising small children was one thing, but really trying to get to know people, to talk with them, to ask questions that might help me understand who they are and how they feel, was another. Not having the power of language is almost like being deaf and mute. Still, the way people move, the tone of their voice, their eyes, all orchestrate a unique sublanguage. Sometimes it is enough.

Ann single-handedly tends to her herd of forty goats, milking them twice a day. Each milking takes two hours. She rises at five in the morning and goes to bed around midnight. When she isn't milking, feeding, or herding her goats, she makes cheese—batches and batches of cheese. Her passion and talent are spent in the creation of flavors and styles that are normally not associated with goat cheese production. For instance, she has developed goat-cheese Gorgonzola, Roquefort, Camembert, blue cheese, and Brie, along with the traditional caprine and a Swedish *getmese*.

Her laboratory for these delicacies is a spotless kitchen. Wearing a freshly laundered plain cotton top and pants (very much like surgical garb), and a kerchief to hold her hair back, it is here that she goes to work. From behind the window that separates her kitchen from the cheese shop, visitors can watch her stir a mixture in the industrial-sized stainless steel-cauldron, or pour milk into the molds. I always felt as if I were viewing a nurse tending newborns at the hospital. Loaves and rounds of cheese rest on a large table until they firm up and can be moved into the walk-in refrigerator. There they will sit until it is time for them to be shipped to various shops and grocery stores around the country.

Ann's success, locally as well as nationally, is testified to by the certificates and awards hanging on the wall behind an ancient-looking cash register. My testimony to her achievement is that even I have eaten her goat cheese—and liked it. In the past, my reaction to being offered goat cheese was to extend my arms, index fingers crossed. The first time we visited Ann, she offered me a slice of caprine, a simple white goat cheese. I felt it would be rude to make gagging sounds, so I took the slice of cheese, and...liked it.

I'm not completely converted, however. Most cheeses, and in particular goat cheeses, are still too rich for my taste, but I do like the caprine heated and topped by cloudberries, feta cheese in salads, and some of the other spiced goat cheeses as well. Lars likes them all. And when he tastes one of the samples Ann passes to him over the counter, he practically breaks into a song and dance. She responds with a knowing smile.

I was usually with Lars when we went to the farm, and he did all the talking. I used this as an excuse to go off and visit the goat barn. There the smell of hay and goats enveloped me. I talked to the buck in his small stall; if he didn't try to nibble or nip me through the bars, I'd scratch the top of his head. Then I'd check in on the egg-laying hens. Sometimes Ann's three-year-old daughter, Kerstin, with braided pigtails and barefoot, walked in and showed me how to feed the buck a few handfuls of hay. All this made me wish I could spend more time on a farm.

The desire goes way back. I have always had a secret interest in country living, even though I was born and raised in the city, the progeny of generations of people who worked behind desks, in classrooms, or on trains. It began early on in high school, by which point my family was living in the suburbs. Nonetheless, I learned how to bake bread, sew quilts, and sew clothes, thinking it would come in handy by the time I found some land and got started.

When I first went to Montana, I thought about raising sheep. They were nice to look at. They were smaller than cattle. You didn't have to slaughter them; you could raise them for their wool. They were short and fairly compact and you could transport them in your pickup... at least that was my idea. Sheep seemed like easy animals to manage. So shortly after I arrived I bought a book entitled *Raising Sheep the Modern Way*. I read chapters with titles such as "Problems of

Pregnant Ewes," "Abnormal Lambing Positions and How to Help," "Pneumonia in Lambs," "Wool Maggots and White Muscle Disease." Soon I realized that 90 percent of the book was about the problems sheep have and suggested that the owner would be up day and night, elbow- and knee-deep in gore and mud, trying to keep them healthy and safe. I closed the book and abandoned my sheep-farming fantasy before I had even looked at a piece of property.

Still, I remain something of a romantic when it comes to the *idea* of farming, living in the country, working in a garden. I admire men and women who farm, in the same way I admire an artist or a chef—or anyone who does something well.

It was with this in mind that I asked Ann Klensmeden whether I could follow her around one day. She agreed. One early August morning, I entered the barn. Goats bleated in anticipation of their milking appointment. The warmth from their bodies mingled with the scent of the buck and the smell of grain and straw and just...and just...as I inhaled the richness of it all I was overcome by a violent fit of sneezing. This alerted Ann to the fact that I had arrived, and she came out from the scrub room, where she had been cleaning and preparing the tubes and containers for the milking. I greeted her, then sneezed some more. Desperate not to appear like a weaker specimen of our gender, I shook my head and waved my hand in a gesture that meant "this is nothing—really, I'm fine," and then I smiled and nodded. Ann smiled back.

I was given a blue jumpsuit, the kind Swedish janitors and mechanics wear, and put on a pair of knee-high rubber boots. I was ready to go to work. Or at least ready to watch Ann work.

She moved swiftly and with purpose. She checked, flushed, and connected hoses. She poured grain, scoop by scoop, into the stanchion bowls. She entered the retaining pen and separated the first eight goats to be milked. They trotted happily past her through the open gate and stepped up on the milking platform, where they put their heads through the stanchions to reach the grain. Ann pulled a bar down that secured the goats in position. Next she flipped a switch, and through a series of chains and pulleys the platform of goats rose to chest level to allow for easy attachment of the milking cups.

Down the row of goats Ann went, wiping their teats with a cloth treated with a cleaning solution, then squeezing a second's worth of milk from each teat. This was to determine whether there was any infection or blockage and to help stimulate milk flow. She flipped another switch. There came the hum of machinery, along with suction sounds at regular intervals. She attached Silicon inflations (rubber milking cups) to the teats, and the process of milking was under way. Depending on age, each goat would produce from one to two gallons of milk per day.

We stood back and watched the goats, making sure the inflations remained securely fastened and that the goats didn't kick each other. We spoke in a combination of English and Swedish. This was the first time we had been able to converse without relying on Lars to translate. Ann was interested in what I thought of living in rural Sweden; I wanted to know if she liked goat farming.

"Montana has almost the same weather as here in Sweden," I told her. "Sports fishing, especially fly fishing, is a much bigger industry in the States than it is here. But interest in Idsjöströmmen is growing all the time."

"I wish I had more time to create cheeses and find their market," admitted Ann.

"It must be nice to have your children here where you work."

"My daughter complains that I work too much. The goats are milked only once a day during the summer vacation, so I can spend more time with my children."

"In the States, when I guided fishermen, I had to be gone day after day for nearly three months. I worried about being away from my son too. Now it is better."

One of the inflations came loose on one of the goats, who seemed to be out of milk as well.

"This one is getting old," she said.

"What happens when they can't produce any more milk?" I asked.

"My husband, Bo, sends them to heaven," Ann replied, and paused to study my face for a reaction. I nodded that I understood.

When the first group of eight was finished, the platform was lowered and the goats were led into a large empty pen. Ann instructed me in how to grain them again. *Easy enough,* thought I. After stepping into the pen with their bucket of food, I closed the gate behind me, and instantly got involved in a goat riot. Struggling to reach their trough, I was squeezed and pushed until I almost ended up, like one of my attackers, on all fours. I did not need a goat obedience class to know that a few well-placed knocks with the knee and several hip checks, accompanied by selected oaths, were called for. The grain was eventually delivered. Ann smiled.

The next bunch to be milked would be mine. Ann brought in eight more goats and they scampered to the platform, heads straining toward the dented metal bowls holding the grain that they craved. I wiped their teats and tried to pinch out some milk, but I had no feel for milking. Ann showed me in a motion that made it look as if she were playing a C scale on the piano. Her fingers rolled down the teat while at the same time her hand gently squeezed. Their milk bags felt hard and as hot as a sunburn. Getting a good hold on a teat filled with so much milk wasn't easy. When I was finally able to get a thin stream of milk to squirt out, I squealed with joy, feeling as if I had just discovered one of the secrets of the universe. Down the row of goats I went, wiping and squirting, briefly but wonderfully living out that old fantasy about being the mistress of a sheep farm.

Maybe I could have managed it. Maybe I have it in me to get up early, tend to animals, and . . .

The last goat I handled rewarded me by farting fully in my face when I leaned under her to attach the milking cups. Then she shat on my arm.

After attaching all the milking cups, I stood back to admire the job. Milk flowed. Goats masticated their grain with benign expressions. Healthy, clean, hardheaded goats. Day in and day out, they ate, slept, and produced milk.

"What happens when a goat gets sick? Do you call a vet?" I asked.

"Well, if they get too sick, Bo sends them to heaven."

After two hours, all forty goats were milked and ready to return to their pasture, where they would graze and wander until about five in the afternoon when, with udders full once again, they would be herded back into the barn.

"You can follow the goats," Ann said.

I opened the gate to the outside corral, and suddenly I was swept up in the rush of escaping goats. A series of chicken-wire fences marked the path around the perimeter of the farmyard to the meadow where the Pippi Longstocking horse grazed. I moved along with the goats as if I were their chaperone on a school field trip, passing by three farmhands working on an addition to one of the houses. They stopped their sawing and hammering and waved. They smiled, said something to each other, then smiled again. Perhaps they thought I was taking some kind of goat therapy. I walked through the meadow and through another gate; I walked until I reached the road, where Ann had erected a chicken-wire fence that could be stretched across the road so the goats could be easily and safely herded through to their pasture. They moved as a flock, pouring through the gate and trotting out to reach the luxurious grasses and flowers on the other side. We closed the gate and stood to admire the herd as it scattered into the field. Then we started back to the barn. Time to make some cheese.

Earlier that morning, Ann had begun a batch of *getmese,* a semisweet cheese with such a soft consistency that it spreads easily on crackers or bread. It has a very special taste and is considered a delicacy. A large vat of *getmese* was bubbling away. It was time to stir it and set it into molds.

Ann put me to work, having given me the surgical garb plus kerchief, and I started stirring with authority. The sweet aroma of the golden brown *getmese* was more like brown sugar than cheese. As soon as the *getmese* thickened I helped pour it into the molds.

"You want to work here?" Ann teased.

Maj entered the shop and gently knocked on the partition window. It was lunchtime.

We entered Ann's parents' home, the one she grew up in with her brothers and sisters. The smell of bread and coffee greeted us at the door. We kicked off our shoes and went into the kitchen. Everyone was seated and had begun eating— all four farmhands plus Maj, and Ann's father, Mats. On the birch kitchen table were three different kinds of bread, a bowl of hard-boiled eggs, herring, beets, potatoes, sliced ham, salad, cereal, milk, jam, honey, lemonade, and, of course, that great Swedish coffee.

The discussion around the table involved—as far as I could tell—the pending shipment of poultry on Friday and questions about how to install the plumbing in the new addition. I happily filled my plate with bread, cheese, herring, and a hard-boiled egg.

Out the window, I could see the black dog resting in the shade of the goat barn. Hens were not scratching about in the driveway. The machinery was still. Inside we broke *knäckebröd* into hand-size pieces and layered beets and herring on top.

The farmhands began shyly speaking to me in English; we conversed using the same mix of English and Swedish Ann and I had used. They were curious about what I thought of living in the Swedish countryside. I got the feeling they were a little surprised at my affection for rural life.

Within half an hour we had left the lunch table and gotten back to work. The heartbeat of the farm began again, the rhythms of hammering and sawing; the goats bleated, the chickens clucked, and the tractor hauled hay for bedding to the chicken barn. At five Lars arrived to pick me up. Ann and her mother waved good-bye as we drove down the driveway, past the meadow, where the goats were in the process of making more milk.

Gimdalen Bachelors

I COME FROM A PART of the world that believes all single people would be much happier if they *just found someone*. We are certain there is something wrong with people who remain unattached, that single people must be unhappy, and that whatever is keeping them from being in a relationship can be handled. Never mind broken hearts or unrequited love—they must give togetherness another chance. We just can't leave well enough alone. So it was perhaps inevitable that I should become curious about the bachelors of Gimdalen.

There are about five men in the village who live alone or

with their mothers, never got married, and have no prospects of doing so in the immediate future. In a community of approximately a hundred souls, and assuming the ratio of men and women is approximately 50:50, that means 10 percent of the adult males in the village live with their mothers. If this can be applied on a national scale, it means approximately five out of every fifty Swedish women with sons (I don't know about the daughters) will never experience empty-nest syndrome.

In Gimdalen, a man can live with his mother without so much as a sideways glance. Living with your mother is more like working a job than like not having a life. Usually he occupies one floor and she the other. They go about living parallel lives and meet for meals, which in most cases she has prepared.

These men didn't appear to be unhappy, so far as I could tell. Some of them went to the barn dances during the summer, where, once in a while, they were rumored to have "gotten lucky." They exercised their hunting dogs, drank a beer or two at the pub, and drove to Bräcke to work. Some of them fished, some of them hunted, some of them fished and hunted. They knew the woods, and the animals and the birds that lived there. They could tell you whether or not it was going to be a good year for blueberries.

I began to see how someone might be content to be a single person in the village. The longer I was there, the more I understood the pleasures of solitude. You get used to the quiet of your day, the lack of interference from the outside world, whose demands and expectations do not reach this place hidden in the forest. You become comfortable with yourself, your schedule, your needs. Being with someone else means having to interrupt the silence, step outside of yourself, converse rather than simply listen—whether to wind rustling birch leaves or a program on TV.

When I met one of the Gimdalen bachelors while out getting the mail or walking in the forest, his shyness was so obvious and painful it was nearly catching. He quickly looked away and scanned the horizon for something interesting to study. As we approached each other, anxiety grew; I could feel it. Neither of us wanted to have to be the first to say *hej,* smile, and nod. We would almost rather have jumped into the ditches at the sides of the road. As we neared each other, I brightened and tried to make contact; he mumbled something back. We managed to acknowledge each other's existence. Then a few steps later we both quietly exhaled with relief.

Nonetheless, how does a grown man end up alone, in the same bed and in the same room he has slept in for over sixty years? Maybe it just happens. Twenty years go by, and then another twenty years, and then another. He is the brother, uncle, or cousin who shows up for the school play, the musical recital, the wedding, and who can always be counted on to bring Mom and then take her home afterward. One day he turns forty. Then fifty. The years carry him along. There are responsibilities to see to: in the spring the roof needs to be fixed; in the summer someone has to cut the lawn; in the fall moose hunting provides food for the table; in winter wood must be chopped and the fire kept lit. Someone has to drive his widowed mother to town for groceries and doctors' appointments. He doesn't have time to question whether his life has enough direction; he's too busy living it. All the other family members have left to start families of their own. But why go when you have someone who needs you, and cooks for you, and who will never leave you? Bachelordom has the conveniences of married life without the emotional demands.

The house we were renting had been lived in by a bachelor, Oskar Rislund. He may even have been born in the house. Oskar and his sister lived here together after their parents died. She had been widowed, and in their advancing age it had made sense for them to keep each other company. Oskar lived his entire life within these walls. As we learned from Carl-Åke, he died quietly on the kitchen sofa of a heart attack one afternoon after working in the yard. He was in his seventies.

There were reminders of Oskar's life throughout the property. Several worn-out articles of his clothing were left in the upper reaches of the shed. Next to the clothing was a collection of empty bottles with crumbling corks—perhaps a long-forgotten stash of moonshine. There was evidence that the shed was also where he processed moose. His large-toothed saws, used when he worked in the forest, hung blackened and rusted on pegs in the two-story barn. Several had his initials stamped on the wooden grips. Four prized moose antlers were mounted on an interior barn wall. In a large wooden chest was a collection of tools necessary to keep a farm running: hammers, nails, files, wrenches, and forging tongs to hold horseshoes in a fire; they were cold and heavy. The leather harness for the horse that pulled felled timber in the woods still carried the sweet sweaty smell of the shoulders it once rested on. The stalls for the milking cows, whose names were apparently Kulla and Kleven, were still standing; a broken porcelain light socket hung precariously overhead. This was where Oskar came in the early morning darkness to feed and milk the cows. I could picture him trudging through the snow, opening the door, and being greeted by the scent of hay and manure and the damp warm air of animals that had been locked in all night. Sitting under that singular dim light, he rested his head against the cow's flank while the sound of steaming milk hit the sides of the tin pail. A slow sun rose later that morning, then slipped back down below the horizon in the early afternoon; and then it was time for the evening's milking.

The house we lived in had been his house, but I felt his presence most in the outbuildings. What belonged to him was in those buildings, and what those things said about him was that he was self-sufficient, a man at home in the woods, responsible to his livestock, and accustomed to hard labor.

Still, I couldn't help wondering why he hadn't started a family of his own. Had he been turned down one too many times at a dance? Did he have bad teeth? Maybe he had the kind of contentment and satisfaction with life that many never find—he was his own best friend.

Elsa Persson had been setting a village record by raising not one bachelor son but four. Elsa's eldest finally married and moved to the old family property at the far end of the village. There, he and his wife began raising their children. But her three other sons remained happily single until that day when, without warning, I'm told, her middle son left for Thailand. Thailand is about as far away from Sweden as you can get and still be on the same planet. Why Thailand? Had Scandinavian Airlines been running a winter getaway special? Perhaps he had recently seen a rerun of *The King and I* and been overcome with romantic notions about "getting to know you." Or maybe, late one night, after everyone else was in bed and the house had grown quiet except for the ticking of the clock in the downstairs kitchen, he had felt life passing him by, tick by tock. No one seemed to know. But when Bengt Persson returned from his sudden trip to Thailand, he returned a married man.

It was the talk of the village for weeks. People smiled and shook their heads. It was such a surprise. The next thing that happened gave the village a collective coronary. Bengt's new Thai sister-in-law flew over for a visit, and his brother Tord fell in love with her! Two Swedish brothers married two Thai sisters, and they began raising their children in Gimdalen.

The remaining bachelor brother didn't rush to the airport; he kept on being a bachelor. Elsa and Stig lived just across the road from Bengt—about fifty feet away to be exact. In her nineties, Elsa was the oldest woman in the village. She was very hard of hearing, and when she talked she shouted as if she were standing beneath the rotating blades of a helicopter.

But on the day I saw her making a rare appearance outside her house, she was planting seeds for the garden with Stig. They didn't speak. A plot of soil had been neatly marked off and tilled on the westerly side of the house—just outside the kitchen window at which Elsa sits all day long, watching the passing of cars and villagers on the main road. Each year her garden produces rows of potatoes, lettuce, cabbage, beets, carrots, dill, strawberries, and rhubarb. She had parked her blue walker—one of those with four wheels, a brake system, and a padded vinyl bench for when walking or standing becomes too much. She had shuffled out to one of the rows, and was standing next to Stig, studying the ground.

Elsa poked holes in the ground with the end of a long

stick. Stig dropped seeds into the holes. He could have left her in the house and done all the planting more quickly by himself; instead, he patiently followed his mother's directions, giving her his arm as they stepped toward the next row. They had their world. It might not be the most adventuresome, the most stimulating, but it was theirs, and they caused no harm. One by one they put the seeds into place, covered them with dirt, and watered them. Hopes for their successful growth into plants went unspoken, as did the understanding that not all of them do.

Surströmming

THE VIKINGS DISCOVERED the new world by riding the open seas in boats about as sophisticated as a canoe. They also invaded and conquered foreign lands, whacked on poor European farmers with double-edged swords, and took property, wives, and daughters that didn't belong to them. It only makes sense that the descendents of these courageous and lawless people continue to show their strength by eating a smelly little marinated fish called *surströmming,* or "sour herring."

On the third Thursday of every August, Swedes crack open a can of *surströmming,* which has been fermenting in a special brine solution for a little over a year. They call this event *surströmmingspremiären*—the sour herring premiere—and it is traditionally a northern Swedish experience. The tins the fish come in bulge from the gases produced during the fermentation process. This is one's first clue that something might not be quite right, particularly if you know a thing or two about botulism. To soften the initial malodorous assault, the cans of sour herring are opened under running water. Outside. In fact, *surströmming* is preferably eaten outside as well, for the walls of the room it is served in will take on its odor for several days. One of our neighbors has built a little cottage especially for this occasion that he calls the *surströmmingsstugan,* or "sour herring cottage."

As the third Thursday of August approached, I was asked by curious villagers, "Are you going to try it?" When I answered yes, they smiled. They knew very well that this would be a kind of initiation. After tasting the herring I would fall into one of two camps: either I would love it or I would hate it. Black or white. Yes or no. There was no middle ground when it came to *surströmming*.

I had heard that watching someone eat *surströmming* for the first time can be highly entertaining. By the time most Swedes have calmly scraped the skin off the herring, removed its bone, and popped the fish into their mouths, most foreigners would have already left the table, green at the gills. Such behavior only makes Swedes grin and continue eating. I was going to be different. I would show them that I was no sissy foreigner.

My approach was to push all negative thoughts away. I would try this fish with an open mind. Breathe in its bouquet. Discuss the spices that went into the marinade. Comment upon the color and texture of the fish, the way its flavor blended with the potatoes and onion. After all, I reassured myself, I liked *inlagd sill* (herring marinated in vinegar and spices). I felt I was halfway there to liking *surströmming*.

I was upstairs in the house when I caught the first whiff. Although Lars had opened the can outside at the water pump, he had left the front door open. I could hear the water running as he rinsed the fish. *Ignore the fact that it smells like garbage on a warm day,* I told myself.

Lars had set the kitchen table and laid it with serving dishes of chopped raw onions, boiled new potatoes, *knäckebröd*, Västerbotten cheese, and a selection of aquavit. I sat down and waited quietly.

Lars put the herring on a plate and placed it in front of me.

"What do I do now?" I asked.

"Watch me," said Lars.

He preferred the time-honored process of using knife and fork to skin the herring, then he skillfully pressed down the fillet and lifted the bone out with his fork. Next he speared a piece of potato and put it on a piece of *knäckebröd*. To that he added the chopped onion. Then, finally, he topped it with a bite of herring. After following his example I paused, a loaded *knäckebröd* in my left hand and a glass of chilled Rånäs aquavit in the other.

"*Skål,*" said Lars.

"*Skål,*" I repeated.

In went the fish, down went the aquavit.

"Aggghhh! Delicious!" exclaimed Lars.

I bit into my herring and potato sandwich, then swallowed the aquavit as fast as I could. The taste of *surströmming* reminded me of petroleum and wood—no, plastic. Then it became earthy, not like soil exactly, but definitely old and logged. It was salty. There was, of course, a strong fishy smell. In short it was like a primary color: there didn't seem to be anything to compare it to. It was what it was.

Lars was already halfway into his second forkful. I could barely finish the first. He went about it quickly and cheerfully. I took shallow breaths. The whole room was awash in the scent of *surströmming*. I tried to take another bite.

"Eat the roe from the female. It's the best part," said Lars, tapping the mass of gray eggs with the tip of his knife. I had just scraped them out of my herring and put them off to the side.

"Okay," I said. I had no intention of eating them.

Because it was the premiere, at least a million people or more were eating *surströmming* that day. Over a million or more people, smiling and toasting and saying, "Agggghhh! Delicious!" then fighting over who would get the roe. There would be contests over who could eat the most. No fewer than seven brands would be open and available to sample in the grocery store. People would talk about *surströmming* on the radio and on television.

I had almost finished a second bite of herring when I knew that I had had enough.

"Are you through?" asked Lars.

"Yes," I replied weakly. "You can have the rest."

He smiled greedily, took my plate, and scraped the remains onto his. I excused myself and went outside. I sat down on the front porch steps and put my head between my knees. I needed oxygen.

The next day we drove to Bräcke to get groceries. I didn't feel particularly well. I kept burping *surströmming* burps. Just as we got out of our car, we ran into an old friend of Lars's. Every time he spoke—I swear—tiny *surströmmings* swam out of his mouth. When the automatic doors of the grocery store slid open, a blast of *surströmming*-soaked air wafted over us. There had been a sampling there the day before. At the bank, the teller boasted about his consumption of an entire can of Oskar's Surströmming. I just stared at him.

For nearly two days, everyplace we went and everyone we met reeked of *surströmming*. I suppose it makes sense. If you are going to do this disgusting thing as a nation you might as well agree to get it over with at the same time. Nobody wants to stand alone in a crowd with *surströmming* breath. In fact, nobody wants much to do with it after the premiere is over. There is no such thing as *surströmming* leftovers. Curiously, what isn't eaten is thrown away, as if it could go bad. And the only people in the world who are eating this stuff are Swedes. Other countries aren't standing in line to import *surströmming*. And if they did they would have to get the shipment by boat. Later that summer we tried boarding a plane with a can of *surströmming* in Lars's carry-on bag and were politely but firmly reprimanded by a security officer, who said with a furrowed brow, "I'm sorry, sir. If we lose pressure in the cabin and this tin comes open . . . it just isn't allowed." Reluctantly, Lars handed it over.

"They're going to have to update their rules on hazardous carry-on items," I remarked, trying to sound sympathetic.

A quick glance at the airline's policy regarding hazardous materials and firearms revealed a ban on "compressed gases, poisons, etiologic agents, radioactive materials and irritating materials."

Lars didn't speak for some time. I took his hand in mine as we waited for the plane to take off.

"Don't be upset," I comforted him. "It's for our own good."

Secrets from the Deep

INGEMAR NÄSLUND, the biologist from the University at Umeå leading the study on the effects of catch-and-release fishing on Idsjöströmmen, showed me how to get into the dry suit. I had been invited to join him and his team while they performed a fish count. The information they gathered would be compared to past counts, to see if the grayling were growing in numbers. The biologists would count as many grayling as they could see, then use that number to calculate the approximate number of grayling in the whole catch-and-release section. To do a proper count, the biologists would float down the river with snorkels on three times per visit and no less than every second month for a year. Their study would show at what time and temperature the grayling migrated into and out of Idsjöströmmen as they moved between the river and Idsjön. Lars and I were eager to learn what the numbers were.

Wearing dry suits, flippers, masks, neoprene gloves, and snorkels, the four biologists and I duck-walked into the river just above the bridge. As if on cue, we plopped facedown into the chilly water; aligned ourselves in a row, and began our float downstream. Unlike a wet suit, a dry suit is watertight; it traps just enough air, so that we could ride the river's current like large pieces of jetsam. After years of struggling in rough water with wading staffs and clumsy thick wading boots, being so careful not to fall in, it was liberating to go with the current rather than to fight it.

As a fly fisher, my insight into a river has always been more or less an interpretive act; I guess at where the trout or grayling lie. Protruding boulders and undercut banks offer clues, not promises, about what might be found beneath the surface. Confidence in knowing where the fish are grows with experience. I trust that there are fish in the deep pools that turn the water dark, or in the riffled runs where so many fish have taken my flies. I rely on what experience has taught me, but I am also an optimist at heart, since I trust in something other than experience. Call it intuition or faith—it sits on my shoulder as I sling line and leader, attached to a fly so small I can hardly see it, into a wall of water I can't see through, to catch a creature I believe is there.

Fishing is mostly a matter of good guessing, like tossing a basketball over your shoulder toward the hoop, or parallel parking, or feeling the wall for a light switch in the dark. I am a little lost until I catch a fish. Then I feel found again. It is a strangely satisfying practice.

Therefore what I saw when I looked down into the river gave me a shock. The underwater landscape was no longer a place where I needed my imagination. No more might be . . . , should be . . . , could be . . . , or looks like maybe . . . , to suggest where to toss a fly. The mask made it possible for me to see, for the first time, what really existed below.

In the clarity of the water and the midday light, I could see the cracks in the stones, different varieties of moss growing on the rocks, and loose debris swirling through the water like a light dust storm. The first grayling I caught sight of did not flee the way I thought it would, the way fish usually do when I thunder up to them, casting my shadow while wading or walking the bank. It held steady behind a rock, where it had probably been all day. I was but a curiosity while it waited for something smaller and more edible to pass by.

The next pool I floated into presented a grayling that was at least twenty-two inches long, one of the largest I had ever seen. I reached for a boulder and anchored myself, so that I could study the grayling's perfect form. We were suspended eye-to-eye; I watched, completely absorbed by the grayling's movements. The fish opened and closed its mouth to feed on nymphs drifting past in the current.

Ingemar floated into sight, and enthusiastically I pointed to the grayling and shouted, "Look at that," which underwater sounded like "blurp blat blat." I even reached for the fish, thinking I might touch it, but of course it sidled away. I released my grip on the boulder and let myself continue to drift in the current.

Rapids swept me over a stone threshold; the water churned and engulfed me in a curtain of bubbles. On the other side of the bubbles was a school of six grayling. Startled by my sudden appearance, they swam in unison in the opposite direction and out of sight.

In the slower sections of the river, logs left over from logging days lay scattered over the river bottom like wreckage from a sunken ship. Some of the pools were filled with fish, others were surprisingly vacant. I came upon another large grayling, noting that when fish were that big they often had a pool to themselves, or if they were in the productive feeding lanes with other grayling, they were first in line for the biggest and tastiest morsels that should float by.

I had a sudden revelation. If I surfaced to mark where I was along the shoreline, I could fish for all the big fish I was seeing. I lifted my head out of the water to memorize the look of the trees, rocks, and any other landmarks that would lead me back to this spot.

A week earlier, Peter and I had been sitting in a rowboat fishing Myssjön, the lake through the woods behind our house, for perch and pike. After a fishless hour Peter told me that he thought what we needed was an electronic fish finder, like one he had seen in a fishing magazine.

"If we had one of those, we could find out where the fish are."

"Just be patient," I had replied.

I had seen ads for electronic fish finders and was mystified by the ad copy. One such ad read:

The old days of looking at moss on logs or examining ripples in the water to figure out the best way to catch fish are gone. For the angler with too little time to wait for divination from nature, PRO FISH gives you the upper hand. This sophisticated unit keeps track of depth and fish size and will even give you the distance to the target so you can judge the next cast. A split screen allows the captain to keep track of the boat's location and the schools of fish below. PRO FISH has three different icons for fish size and an alarm to make sure you're paying attention. Everything Ahab could have used to even the score.

The ad suggested that fishing was a chore, and that anything to help you get through the experience efficiently and painlessly was welcome. These gadgets sell like crazy but I can't fathom why. Even when the sonogram technician traced the shape of my child as it swam onto the screen and asked whether I wanted to know if it was a boy or a girl, I had stated emphatically *no*. I didn't want a machine spoiling my fun. Anticipation was part of the experience.

I'm not alone. There's Clyde. I never actually met Clyde, but I once ended up sitting next to his wife, a housewife in her late sixties, on a plane. As soon as she found out that I liked to fish she told me all about her husband.

"Every day, when we are at our summer cabin, Clyde goes down to the lake and casts off our dock. Sometimes he's there for hours and doesn't catch a thing. One day he'd been out about five hours and he hadn't moved and he hadn't caught a thing, and I walked down to the dock and asked him, 'Why do you torture yourself? Why don't you come in?' and he said, 'Because I'm waiting for the damn fish to bite.' "

It's hard to explain this kind of patience to a six-year-old. Peter still wanted the gizmo and was in the middle of asking me again to consider getting him one when suddenly his rod tip jerked dramatically. Something heavy, strong, and alive was on his line.

"I got one. *I got one!*"

After ten minutes of my hollering directions about holding the rod tip up, letting the fish run, and reeling, Peter finally wrestled an eight-pound pike to the boat.

"See, you don't need a fish finder, you *are* a fish finder!" I told him.

The most exaggerated electronic fish-finding device I ever heard of was once explained to me by a man who worked for the European Union patent office in Belgium. He had recently helped a client complete patenting procedures for his fiberoptic fish finder. The fiberoptic fishing line transmitted pictures back to a small screen, so you could see what was coming in to take your lure. If you thought the fish was too small you could push a button that sent an electric shock to the hook and frightened the fish away. If the fish was a record-breaking catch, once it had hold of the hook, you could push the same button and stun it for easy retrieval. A person didn't even have to risk getting a hernia bringing it in. In addition with this device a fisher would be able to see the one that got away.

How sad, I thought. No more guessing by the way water moved or changed color where fish might be. No more relying on intuition and experience. No more wondering about the size of the lunker that got away. No more lucky fishing hat.

Continuing down the river with Ingemar and his colleagues, I remained fascinated by this view of the secret life of fish. The aquatic plants rooted in the sandy bottom reached up and waved, like arms swaying at a revival meeting. The fish remained calm and certain of their place—not anxious and thrashing as they would be after I'd dragged them up into the biting air. And except for the sound of my breathing through the snorkel, it was quiet. Extremely quiet. My movements were slower and calmer than on land. I felt buoyant and light. I lost interest in my plan to mark places where the bigger fish lurked. I quit surfacing. I enjoyed simply being with the fish.

The Moose Hunt

IN RURAL SWEDEN, events are referred to by whether they happen before or after the moose hunt. Almost half the workforce is away from the job during opening week in September. You hope your car doesn't break down and your plumbing doesn't back up, because unless you are a moose or a hunting dog, you won't get any attention.

This annual drama is rich in traditions, camaraderie, lore, and rites of passage. Each year new chapters get written as younger members rise up to try their luck and display their skill. Older chapters about legendary hunters and their prowess are recalled. The hunt has its practical side too—the meat will feed families through the winter.

Hunting moose is a team effort. Gimdalen has two teams, with ten to fifteen members on each. Team members are normally either landowners or people who lease land in designated hunting areas. A member inherits membership, or acquires it through the purchase of property that includes hunting rights. Someone must retire, die, or sell his rights before a new member can join, and this new member must pass a rigorous hunting exam, as well as pay fees to both the county and the team.

Specialists keep hunting teams throughout Sweden informed about moose populations in every district. Based on that information, each team decides how many moose will be taken in their area. In the Gimdalen area, permission to take up to sixteen moose was not unusual.

Once a moose has been killed, all the team members join in to help field-dress it and transport it back to the village. All moose taken in a day are hung by that evening.

The antlers and the hearts go to the hunters who shot them. The skins are kept or sold. Bones are placed in a pile in the forest. Meat is equally distributed. Excess meat is sold to villagers.

Each team has a leader. He decides when the day's hunt begins and when it ends, where it will take place, and from which direction the *Jämthunds* (medium-sized gray-and-white hunting dogs that look like cousins of the husky, named for the area where they are bred) will be walked. He oversees the drawing of lots that determines which stands will be assigned to which hunter. He is also responsible for counting kills, or deciding when a hunter has fired but missed and whether or not that shot should count as a kill. This rule is designed to inspire accuracy and to curb trigger-happy hunters, but it can make for a few tense moments when a hunter's actions are put under review.

Hearing so much about this hunt piqued my curiosity. I wanted to go. I didn't want to shoot—just watch. Bengt, who had been a team leader for the past twenty years, said I could accompany him.

The moose hunt has been sanctioned by the women whose men are participating.

"It is better that he go away for a week. Stay at our *stuga* in the forest. There he can be with his friends, drink, stay up late. I don't want to see him until it is over," said one woman.

But another complained that somehow another week had been added to the moose hunt this year, meaning that her husband would be gone every weekend in September and half the weekends in October.

DAY 1

I rose at five. Barely awake, I shuffled to the kitchen, where the woodstove roared with a well-stoked fire. Lars pushed a cup of hot tea into my hand, then flipped the eggs one last time, buttered the toast, and poured milk on the oatmeal, before setting it all in front of me at the table. Leaving the cozy kitchen for the cold outdoors was going to be difficult. Lars also made me a thermos of tea and a sack lunch. He checked what I wore, fussed over the layers of clothing I had on, and insisted I put on more. He checked my camera gear and tied a rain jacket to the top of my day pack, where I could easily reach it. At fifteen minutes to six, after being hugged and kissed, I stepped off the front porch of our house.

"Good luck," Lars said, "and be careful."

Twenty steps away I turned around. "I can't believe I'm going hunting."

Lars answered with a smile. I knew he would watch me until I disappeared from view.

Five minutes later, I arrived at Bengt's house, and knocked. When the door opened I felt awkward. I was unsure whether I should go inside or stay out on the front step. Bengt motioned me in. As I crossed the threshold, we shuffled and collided. Deciding it would be better to wait by the car, I backed out of the doorway. I figured that Bengt needed time to finish last-minute tasks. He could mutter to himself about misplaced socks and ammunition without having to worry about an audience in his living room.

Finally Bengt emerged from his house with a backpack and his 30/06 Husquevarna rifle. We piled into his blue 1989 Saab 900, which his brother had sold to him. Spots of rust showed where paint had been chipped by numerous trips down rural roads, and there were three places on the windshield where rocks had left jagged, expanding cracks. A coat of dust lay over the dashboard. An odd assortment of coins lay in the center divider, alongside a nearly empty Tic-Tac box. A week's worth of discarded mail and shopping flyers were tucked between the seats and scattered on the floor.

Dawn was upon us when we pulled out onto the village's main road, which was relatively packed with cars. Everyone was in a hurry. No one wanted to be late.

On Idsjöströmmen's bridge, most of Bengt's team had already assembled. They looked as if they had been waiting for some time. When I stepped from the car, some of the men smiled and greeted me with a nod. Bengt took out a briefcase and clipboard and set up shop on the hood of his Saab. The team gathered around while he gave out instructions. When a young hunter arrived five minutes late, the others simultaneously pulled up sleeves and looked at their watches. Someone said something and a low rumble of laughter followed. The young hunter stared at his feet.

Next, playing cards were pulled from a deck. This is how the hunters draw their positions. Pulling a queen means you get last pick. As they looked at their cards, a few grumbled, others looked pleased, but in the end everyone was clear about his position. The team would break for lunch at one, and meet up at the fire ring located on the road to Åsberet.

Before Bengt and I drove off, I was given my hatband, a hunter-orange ribbon used for safety and for identification. Carl-Åke helped pin it on. He was like a prom date fumbling with my corsage. The orange ribbon meant that I was marked. Everyone in the village would understand what I was doing. It made me feel I belonged.

After a short drive, Bengt pulled over. Without explanation, he went to his trunk and gathered up his gear and rifle. He didn't lock the car, but did insist on checking my door, to make sure I had shut it all the way.

"Now we will walk," he announced.

I thought this might be a kind of test. Could I keep up with an experienced hunter? Could I manage the terrain? Would I need my asthma inhaler? We started to walk. I knew that the moment we entered the forest I shouldn't make any noise. No talking. No crinkling candy wrappers. No stepping on fallen branches.

I was reminded of the concerts my mother used to take me to as a young girl. She had a thing for the classical guitarist Andrés Segovia, and when I was about eight we went to one of his concerts in San Francisco. She warned me that he would not begin if anyone was talking, coughing, or fanning herself with her program. In fact, he would reprimand the offending person from the stage, or simply get up and leave. I was so terrified I could hardly listen to Segovia play. I was afraid to clear my throat, or that I might sneeze. He would search me out in the audience and stare me down, and all those well-dressed, respectable people my parents' age would turn and look and blame me for ruining their concert. I walked very quietly behind Bengt.

Bengt soon stopped, put his pack down, loaded his rifle, clicked on the safety, and struck a relaxed standing pose. He studied the sloping terrain before us. Once the dogs began to move and stirred things up, this was where moose could be expected to cross. Bengt whispered to me to put my pack down, which I did. Then I stood quietly, looking where he was looking.

Waiting is part of being a sportsman. Over the years I have come to the opinion that the bigger the animal you are interested in making contact with, the longer the wait. I am used to waiting. Fishing requires a lot of waiting. I could wait. But I secretly hoped something would hurry up and happen.

Once we settled in at our post I realized how utterly and completely quiet it was. I could hear Bengt breathing, which meant that he could probably hear me breathing too. Then my stomach growled. I wondered whether Bengt regretted bringing me along. If you're out alone you don't have to hold back gas or care about a growling stomach. If you're out hunting with someone you don't know that well, especially if you're someone else's girlfriend, well, you can't be yourself really. I worried that some curious sound might escape from either one of us, embarrassing the other. The thought kept me on edge.

Despite being on the alert for the odd noise, little by little I began to feel comfortable about our silence. The only sounds came from chirping birds, and the wind blowing, making trees creak with their swaying. Something changes when there is no talk. Something within becomes still and more aware. You gain a greater sensitivity to sound, motion, and color. You start to *feel* the place you're in. Much is understood without explanation.

We stood silent for two hours. Then we heard a rifle shot echoing in the distance. Bengt fumbled for his radio, as if reaching to silence an alarm clock after a deep sleep. He turned it up to hear the patter of conversation. His brother's guest from Stockholm had shot a large bull moose. They were just over the hill from us. Ten points on the antler. No rushed excited voices, no long-winded story, merely a matter-of-fact exchange of information. Bengt spoke briefly to his brother, then put the radio away. We went back to standing and waiting.

As planned, we broke for lunch precisely at one, joining the rest of the team at the fire ring. Several coffeepots were resting on burning coals. Some of the hunters joked with each other, others quietly ate their lunch or gazed into the fire. The guest from Stockholm was the one with bloodstains on his rubber boots. I congratulated him. He smiled. I tried to get him to tell the story, but sensed his reluctance, then realized that his success was not being discussed. Thinking that I might be breaking some kind of code of humility, I stopped asking questions. Still, I was curious to see the moose he had shot.

After lunch the team decided to move to another location. Again we drove only a short distance, and got out of the car.

"We will walk," said Bengt.

Again I prepared myself for a hike. We walked for less than five minutes into the forest.

"Here," he said, and we stopped.

Being together was getting easier. We even talked a little. Bengt was more relaxed and less adamant about standing stone-still in one spot. I felt comfortable enough to sit on the ground. After an hour, Bengt offered to take my picture. We started taking pictures of each other holding the rifle, posing as if we were hunting.

Suddenly the radio crackled. Roger, one of the dog handlers, let us know he was nearby. We immediately returned to our post. I strained to hear any sounds. As I listened I felt something change, something in the atmosphere of the place, which I can only describe as a vibration. Roger's *Jämthund* jumped out of the brush into the open in front of us just as I was about to tell Bengt that I thought I'd heard something. The dog ignored us. It went on sniffing and panting, nose to the ground, craving the scent of moose then disappeared back into the brush. I could not see Roger. This made me wonder whether he might get in the way of a bullet, though I assumed that those kinds of problems had already been worked out.

About twenty minutes later, again something shifted—something in the air—in the trees. Something was coming. Then they were there. A moose calf and its mother.

They burst out of the woods and trotted into the clearing before us. There they froze. Looking vulnerable and confused, they attempted a retreat. Bengt readied himself and aimed. The mother turned sideways, presenting her chest. Bengt didn't shoot. The calf remained sideways, opposite its mother. The mother leaped back into the woods. The gun went off. I thought Bengt would fire again because it looked as if he had missed. The calf took a hobbled step and fell.

Bengt waited. He listened. Then he started to walk toward the calf. I followed. I touched Bengt's shoulder to get his attention and patted my ear, for I had heard something. He looked at me, his face a question mark. Then came a sound, like a cry, and chillingly I understood it was the mother moose, calling. Bengt heard it too. I got behind him as he readied the rifle for the mother's return. We waited.

The brush and leaves remained still. Like smoke rising, excitement dissipated. Bengt shook his head. He said that once the cow sensed danger she would leave. Later she might call for the calf when she felt it was safe, but it was the calf's job to keep up with her.

The calf was on its side, kicking its back legs. It struggled to get up and run. Its large brown eyes were like polished stones, settled in a bed of long lashes. The neck strained to pull the front legs up. The calf rocked, then rested, then kicked. For a minute she lay quiet and I thought it was over. Bengt nudged her shoulder with his hand. She kicked and rocked some more.

"I will take another," Bengt said quietly.

"Yes. Yes, I understand," I said, and moved away, thinking I wouldn't look.

I thought he would stand back farther, but he got right up to the calf, placed the barrel of the gun at the back of the head, and squeezed the trigger. The calf's legs stiffened, then were seized with a tremor, then slowly relaxed. I saw all this from behind Bengt. Part of me started to float away. The calf's coat was smooth. I knelt down and stroked its side.

Bengt called out on his radio to let the others know. His nephew radioed back that he would come help. I thought something else was supposed to happen. I thought maybe some last words would be appropriate. Every pet I had ever had as a child—from goldfish to hamsters—had been given a cardboard coffin and funeral service before being buried in our backyard.

Bengt rolled the calf over and pointed.

"It is a female," he said.

Then he felt around at the base of its rib cage and pushed gently. He found the place to make the incision and began to cut. I saw that I could help Bengt by pulling back on one of its legs, so I did. Immediately the bottom of a black hoof was in my face, mud and moss were jammed into its cloven crevice, smelling of moist, dark woods. I thought of the moss and mud stuck to the bottom of my son's tennis shoes after he had been in the forest.

Bengt wanted to get the animal dressed quickly, but unfortunately the shot had nicked the stomach. No one wants to be up to his elbows in stomach contents; the bacteria found there can contaminate the meat. Plus the odor is just about intolerable.

The smell of blood was in the air. It felt warm, even in one's nostrils. I didn't mind looking at it, but I wanted to keep my distance. I thought of that old myth about how women handle the sight of blood better than men because they see it every month, and because they've seen it on newborn children, and on their children's cuts and scratches. None of that helped me here. This was gallons of blood, not thimbles.

Leif arrived. Like engineers, they worked on solving the problem of swift and easy gut removal. I circled their operation, wishing I could be more helpful, do something constructive, but felt I'd only get in the way. I stood off to the side, like a member of a patient's family waiting in the lounge for word from the doctor. Finally—success, the white sacks that contained the stomach and intestines were rolled onto the forest floor, where they would provide a feast for birds and scavengers.

Bengt and Leif explained that they wanted to hang the calf up by the hind legs, to drain off the rest of the blood and work on some stubborn organs that wouldn't come out. Leif made a cut in each hind leg between the Achilles' tendon and the leg bone, which we threaded with a branch. Together Leif and I hoisted her up and carried her over to a tree. She was over two hundred pounds. This would have been the last winter she would have spent with her mother. We sank beneath her weight but managed to press into the tree and hold her up while Bengt finished the dressing.

The part of me that had excused herself earlier continued to swim around, like a vapor, close enough for me to know that she hadn't disappeared entirely, but far enough away for me to feel disconnected. After Bengt got the heart out he stuck it on top of a small fir, like the star on a Christmas tree. We lowered the calf to the ground. I walked over to the fir and touched the heart. It was firm. It felt strong and healthy.

I could sense that Bengt was tired. He confessed that he did not like the shot he had taken. He felt badly about it. But he had done everything else right. Should a moose cow appear first, you must wait to see how many young are with her. If she has only one calf, the calf must be taken first, then the cow. If a cow appears with two young, only one of the calves may be taken. Though the cow had presented Bengt with the best shot, he had waited and taken the calf first. He was a good hunter.

I asked if it bothered him to shoot a calf.

"No," he said.

He added that many of the older hunters in the village did not like to take calves. The meat was desirable and tender, but there was something about it they did not care for. He was not able to tell me what it was exactly that bothered them.

We had to drag the calf out to the road and get it back to the village, so we put a rope around its neck and dragged the carcass the hundred yards to the dirt road Bengt and I had walked in on. Two other hunters, Martin and Carl-Åke, met us. Bengt went to get his car.

It became obvious that the calf was too big for the trunk of the Saab. The hunters discussed how to manage the rest of the calf's journey to the village. It was quickly decided. Off went the head.

I did not grimace in disgust. No grief. No protest. I was only a receptor. I took in the scene to study later, so that I could try and understand what it meant. But already there was a restless thought that insisted on surfacing and resurfacing: that a creature who had been suckling its mother, tripping through the grass behind her, and mewling less than an hour earlier was now being taken apart like a jigsaw puzzle. Martin picked up the severed head by the ears. I did not think he should hold it like that. I was afraid the ears would tear off. He shifted his weight as if to swing a sack of grain and tossed the head into the forest. It landed at the base of a fir, upright, like a headstone. I wondered if they shouldn't have buried it. What if its mother returned? I said nothing.

One by one the legs were tossed after it, the mud and moss still clinging to the hooves, still damp from the morning's dew. What was left of the calf was shrouded in plastic, tossed in the trunk, and driven to the team's processing barn, where they skinned it, wrapped it in protective netting to keep flies off, and hung it next to the bull moose that had been taken earlier that morning.

The moose reminded me of the great sides of beef I would sometimes see hanging in the cooler at the neighborhood market where I grew up. Jimmy the meat cutter, as we called him, was the butcher. Behind Jimmy's butcher block was the door to the giant cooler, where he hung and aged the beef. He let me follow him there sometimes so that I could get a good look at the carcasses. They were red and white and only like a cow in an abstract way. Behind the big glass front of Jimmy's display case, various animal parts rested in special compartments bordered by fresh parsley. People still ate variety meats, like tongue, kidney, liver, heart, sweetbreads, tripe, and pigs' feet. Interest in these meats was dwindling, but they were still available. Once, Jimmy removed a cow's tongue from the case and held it out on a piece of white butcher paper so I could see it better. He laughed when I stuck my tongue out in disgust.

I lingered awhile outside the processing barn, observing the hunters as they worked and watching the villagers who had come to hear about the day's events. One woman's dog strained at its leash, trying to get closer to the butchering. A hunter took pity and dropped one of the bull moose's leg bones at the dog's feet. Two retired hunters stood in the doorway of the shed and quietly exchanged comments. A few women walked over from their houses. Village children arrived throughout the afternoon on their bikes.

A two-year-old boy and his older girl cousin embraced and petted the decapitated head of the bull moose. Soon, the guest hunter who had shot it and been awarded the rights to the antlers stepped up and calmly began skinning the skull, preparation for the boiling and cleaning it would need so he could have the antlers mounted. The children watched, fascinated.

Late in the afternoon, just as I was leaving for home, Bengt approached me.

"Do you want to come tomorrow?" he asked shyly.

"Yes," I answered.

"Even if it rains?"

"Yes."

"Six o'clock?"

"Six o'clock."

DAY 2

I waited in the Saab while Bengt unleashed Stella, his *Jämthund*. Stella had suffered a mysterious illness the day before that had left her unable to stand. Bengt had given her aspirin, and by morning she could walk and in general seemed much improved. But I wondered how well she really was.

A worn blanket had been placed on the backseat for Stella. On command she bounded toward the car and jumped into the back, panting and squirming. I welcomed her using the high-pitched baby talk I use when talking to dogs, before realizing she had probably never heard baby talk in her life. She jumped between the front seats and tried to get on my lap. We started a shoving match.

"Get back!" I commanded her, which was just about as ridiculous as the baby talk, because she didn't respond to commands in English.

Bengt finally rescued us.

"Gor lägdet" (lie down), he said sternly.

She jumped into the backseat and stayed there.

The Saab rattled over the potholes as we drove down the main road of the village while the morning light slowly grew in the east. Panting heavily in the backseat, Stella made wet nose marks across the windows. She seemed to sense the importance of the day. It would be her first hunt.

"Do you think Stella is all right?" I asked Bengt.

He hesitated. "Yes, but she is young."

If Stella was going to make a good hunting dog she was going to have to work. She wasn't a pet. At a year and six months of age, after an entire summer of exercise and preparation, she was assumed to be ready.

The drawing for positions took place, and the hunters left for their various destinations. There would be two dogs working that day: Bengt and I with Stella, and Roger with his dog.

We dog handlers were to wait twenty minutes, allowing the hunters time to establish their positions, then head off, Bengt and I in one direction, Roger in another.

We began by walking the trail along Idsjöströmmen, the one that led to the second windbreak, where some of the best fishing and gatherings of the summer had occurred. As we walked I felt a familiar quiet and coolness settle in, reminding me of the change of seasons that was now in progress. The landscape seemed to be concentrating, so that it could focus on what was ahead.

Stella was released off her lead at the second windbreak. Nose to the ground, she trotted away, knowing exactly what it was she had come to do. The secret voices of her ancestors told her it was moose she must be after. Depending on how clearly she heard those voices, she would know how to charge the moose quietly until, surprised, it ran. Then, barking, Stella would need to continue chasing it until, out of irritation and curiosity, the moose stopped, turned, and lowered its head at her in agitation. This would mean Stella knew how to *stand* a moose. She would have forced the animal to stop its flight, made it pause to confront the source of the bark. When a Jämthund stands a moose, a hunter has the best opportunity to take position, aim, and bring the animal down with a single shot.

Stella looked eager, her tail and ears at attention, her body in constant motion. As we turned off the trail by the river and headed into the woods, Stella went wild with barking, then dashed off. Bengt didn't run after the dog. He just stood and listened. The barking began to grow fainter. Bengt shook his head.

"She is young," he said.

After radio contact with a nearby hunter, we learned that Stella had chased a cow and calf across a clearing. Stella returned to us and received praise from Bengt, not because she had performed well but because she had returned. Jämthunds often disappear during a hunt; and it sometimes takes days before they are found.

Stella continued moving ahead of us, sniffing and investigating and trying to catch a whiff of moose. After another hour, Bengt insisted that she was moving slowly. He was certain it was from the illness the previous day. I suggested that maybe it helped her to think, to pick up scent better. Bengt didn't respond.

We walked through a corridor of birch and firs that circumvented a large marsh, over a mile wide and a mile long. Moose thrive in open areas like marshes and clear cuts. One of their greatest food sources consists of young pine tops. Grasses, birch, and willow also grow here. Moose usually only feed in the open or exposed areas at night. During the day, they make themselves scarce by resting under the cover of the brush and forest that border the clear cut or marsh.

We began to see more and more signs of moose as we went. Hoof prints in the soft dark mud, moist droppings, freshly broken willow branches chewed short. Bengt would point at each sign and I would nod with understanding. Stella began moving more quickly, sniffing fervently, as if inhaling every molecule of moose that clung to leaf, twig, or clump of earth. We also became more alert.

Stella, with ears up, silently bounded off into the woods and disappeared. We heard her barking. Within seconds, five hundred feet away, a bull moose appeared. He seemed to have risen directly from the forest floor and, like a great ship, moved with grace and speed and power. I thought he was running away from us, heading for the creek off to our left. Bengt prepared to shoot. I stepped back and raised my camera. It was the only thing I could think to do.

Something made the moose shy away from the creek. Within seconds he had changed direction. Now he was charging toward us. The sound of branches snapping under his hooves grew steadily louder as he approached. My legs felt the vibration of his pounding steps. I centered the image of Bengt in my viewfinder, getting all of him in sight. In my left eye, the moose ran from the shelter of the forest, and in my right eye, he entered the camera frame. The flash from my camera exploded just as Bengt took his shot.

The moose took several steps, stumbled, and crashed nose-first, like a plane, into the ground. No one said a word. The moose made one or two weak kicks with its back leg. It groaned. Bengt carefully crept toward the moose. I followed.

"Will you need to take another shot?" I whispered.

"No, it's dead."

It groaned a few more times, then took its last shallow breaths. Then it was still.

The final leap, from life as a wild creature into our lives, with gunpowder and flashbulbs, had come suddenly and unexpectedly, as had unexplored feelings of my own. In the instant before the gun had gone off, something in my being had awakened. When I had seen the moose, magnificent in its flight, I wanted to get it. *Get it, Bengt! Shoot it!* was what I had silently begged. Some unknown part of myself came forward, driven neither by guilt nor fear, and joined in the chase.

Bengt used the radio to let the team know he had taken

a bull. Suny, Bengt's older brother, appeared. They talked softly while field-dressing the animal. I stood by the moose's head and petted his nose, although I felt as if I were trespassing. This creature would never have permitted this in life. Still, the muzzle was soft and pliable like the lips of a horse. The hair that covered it was brown, smooth, and shiny. I stroked the nose, smoothing the hair over and over again, then I rested my hand on it. It felt the way a bed does just after its occupant has risen for the day. The moose's nose warmed my cold hand.

After lunch, the rest of the team came with a specially designed all-terrain vehicle that sounded like a lawn mower and had treads like a tank. They secured the moose onto the machine by attaching a wire cable around the base of its antlers and cranking it up into position with a winch, the same way a drift boat is pulled up onto its trailer. The moose traveled on its back, facing the sky. The driver guided the vehicle over the rough contours of the marsh. It might have been a labor-saving device, but it wasn't necessarily a time-saver. First the vehicle became stuck and everyone had to help push. Then something went wrong with the engine, and someone had to make an adjustment to get it going. And then it got stuck again. When it wasn't stalled or stuck, we walked slowly behind it, as in a funeral procession. Bengt carried the animal's heart on a willow branch.

Later that winter I would remember the moose during its last seconds, and how I had turned to face it. I would remember the sound of its hooves pounding, and that Bengt had not hesitated. His reflexes and hunting instincts quickly found the heart of the animal because he had known and understood it all his life. I would remember some dormant part of myself, located somewhere deep in the spine, awakening, grasping the primal balance between survival and death. I told the story and talked to other hunters about what I saw. Remembering and recalling what happened during the hunt helped me to preserve it. Because the hunt must be remembered, and the stories told again and again, to keep them all alive—the day and the moose and ourselves.

House for Sale

WE SAT ACROSS from each other at the kitchen table, whose short legs meant that every time we slid into our chairs the table's wooden apron hit our knees. You might have thought that after weeks of knocking into it we'd have learned to approach it sideways, but we always forgot. It had become a kind of joke. The first person at breakfast would start off the day by banging his or her knees and shouting, "OUCH!" Anyway, there we were one evening, surrounded by the avocado-green wallpaper with the cabbage-sized daisy print, and with knees carefully tucked under the treacherous table, sipping a glass of wine and enjoying the quiet of a late dinner together. Peter was asleep. It was time to talk.

"How do you feel about coming back to Sweden?" Lars began.

I looked around the room. I thought about all those un-usually cold summer nights; about the mosquitoes that had come in through the cracks by the thousands; about how we had slept on a mattress on the floor for nearly three months; about how an outhouse was our bathroom, and the only shower was a half-mile away at the ex-brother-in-law's. The lake had been too cold to swim or bathe in, except for maybe one day; we hung our clothes on a clothesline in the attic as both a place to store them and a place to dry them after we washed them by hand at the water pump in hand-numbingly cold water. And there wasn't a comfortable chair in the place.

Lars wore the seriousness of his question like a business suit. And in that moment he once again endeared himself to me, with his sincerity. He had a way of encouraging me to speak without feeling intimidated. He wanted an honest re-sponse. After all, we were discussing our future.

"I couldn't stand to see everything you've worked for dis-appear. I like the challenge of Idsjöströmmen. I like this change in my life. I like it for Peter too. But mostly I like sharing our lives. One less fishing guide in Montana will not be missed. We can do this. I want to come back to Sweden."

Lars reached across the table. Our fingers threaded to-gether and squeezed tight, in affirmation.

"There's only one thing I'd like to change," I added.

"What's that?" he asked.

"Do you think we could find a place with a shower?"

After making a few inquiries, we discovered there were

no other places to rent in the village, and thus were faced with spending another summer in the same house. Lars called to make arrangements with the owner, Edith Winnberg, who quickly designated her son-in-law, Ivar, to handle the matter. Ivar came over two days later to finalize an agreement.

Lars called Ivar "The Mayor of Gimdalen" because of his trustworthiness and ability to lead. Ivar grew up down the road from Gimdalen in the village of Nyhem, and married Edith Winnberg's daughter, Kerstin. They had three lovely daughters. Ivar was in his fifties, had graying hair and an open, friendly face. He always spoke clearly and carefully, and always meant what he said. He worked for the county, and spearheaded many of the campaigns to inject new life into the rural area in and around Gimdalen. He supported Lars when the fishing board was debating whether or not to lease Idsjöströmmen. Ivar saw tourism as a chance to save the depressed economy. He had fought hard for change and growth.

We met at our kitchen table, cringing when Ivar was the first to bang his knees. Our conversation began with Ivar apologizing for his English. I insisted he speak to Lars in Swedish, and said I would signal when I needed a translation. Key nouns, the tones of their voices, and body language clued me in to everything else. Lars explained that we were staying with the river project and that we needed to rent the house again. Ivar looked interested. Then Ivar said something that sounded like a question. Lars paused, and said, "*Nej*" (no).

Ivar responded as if he were trying to explain something. Again Lars paused. Then Ivar spoke, pointing his index finger as if to tick off points on a list. There was a lull in the conversation.

"*Nej* what?" I asked Lars.

Lars turned toward me.

"Ivar wants to know if we want to buy the house. I think we should rent it for another year or two and find out if—"

"How much do they want?"

Ivar watched us, his eyes moving back and forth, scanning our faces. Lars posed the question. Ivar responded with a figure. It sounded high, but then numbers in Swedish kronor always sounded high to me; at the time, eight kronor equaled a dollar. Lars turned and told me the figure in English. I got my calculator and worked the rate of exchange. I tried not to smile. I asked Lars if it was the right figure. Was he sure?

"Yes, that is the price."

I looked directly at Ivar, "What do you get for this price?"

He answered to Lars in Swedish.

"The house, the barn, the shed, and an acre of land," Lars translated.

I was astonished. The price was so low we could have put it on our Visa card. I tried not to look delighted, but I was. I can't get a deal to save my life. If I ever get a discount on anything it's completely by accident. But as my father used to say, "Even a blind pig gets an occasional acorn." And that decaying house in Sweden was the acorn of my life. At least that was how I saw it.

"Can we see the boundaries?" I asked.

We walked the perimeter of the property, which featured fir, pine, and birch trees. It also featured several underground springs that seeped up to the surface and made the land soggy and damp—a haven for wildflowers and stinging nettles, and, of course, mosquitoes. The buildings had been constructed on the southern end of the property, which was higher and dryer.

The northern boundary was a crumbling stone wall. Bertil and Gudrun's house was behind it to the east, and beyond that the vast forest. Carl-Åke and Maud lived at the end of the road to the west, and just beyond their house was the main road.

Ivar explained that his wife's family had carried the burden of property taxes, new roofing, and upkeep for many years. None of them wanted to live there. The grandmother had been the last occupant, and she had died five years earlier. Before that, the house had been home to two generations of loggers and forest workers.

The hinges on the woodshed door creaked open. Rays of light slipped in through the cracks, illuminating the fact that the shed needed another injection of wood. In the barn were the dried-out leather harnesses and bridles; rusted horseshoes hung on pegs, relics of the days in the early part of the century when horses were used to haul timber and plow potato fields. Cobweb-covered cowbells were ghostly reminders of Oskar's milking cows.

The whole place would continue to fall apart from neglect unless someone came in and took it over. As Lars and Ivar walked and talked, I sensed that Ivar was, in his careful way, explaining the pluses and minuses of the old house. It needed work, no question. It had not been formally put up for sale, but if Lars and I needed a house, we should seriously consider it. Lars listened with guarded interest. Returning to the front porch I was filled with excitement, which I was still trying to contain.

"Let's buy it," I said as soon as Ivar had left.

When someone becomes enthusiastic about a large purchase, especially as large as a house, it is their loved one's duty to try and slow them down, to at least try to make them see the problems that lie ahead—because there will always be problems. Lars explained that the purchase price wasn't such a savings, considering the expense of making the house fit for habitation. He wanted me to understand that we would probably never have the chance to sell it for what it would be worth, even after all the repairs and remodeling.

For just as many reasons why we shouldn't buy the house, I found reasons why we should, the strongest being that since we had decided to stay with Idsjöströmmen, we had to make sure nothing kept us from our duties to the river. Buying a house meant we had made a commitment. We were going to make a life together in the United States and in Sweden. It was perfectly clear to me, after meeting with Ivar, that we had to own the house—drafts, outhouse, unfinished attic, and all. And by the end of August we did.

Home

BY EARLY SEPTEMBER the mosquitoes had disappeared and the birds had quieted. Idsjöströmmen, like a spawned salmon, had lost its vitality. The water levels had dropped and the river was calmer, easier to wade. The boulders and rocks, hidden all summer by a constant flow, now protruded like bones. The pools had become well-defined pockets. The grayling hunkered low in the coolness of their depths.

The water temperatures were still high from the August heat, causing the grayling to feed less and to be less active than before. Crisp fall days and longer nights would lower the water temperature and inspire the grayling to feed again, and in early October, as the chill of fall set in, they would slip like ghosts from their hiding places in the river and migrate upstream, where they would spend the winter in Idsjön.

I too was living between the seasons of coming and going. It was time for me to fly back to Montana with Peter, so that he could rejoin his classmates at school, and I could prepare for the off-season work of speaking engagements and writing assignments. Lars would stay in Gimdalen through September to watch over the river and to take care of late-season fly fishers. By the end of the month, when the grayling were safely on their way to the lake, Lars would leave for the States and we would all be together again. I got the soft canvas luggage out of the barn, dusted it off, then left it sitting empty at the foot of our bed. I could barely bring myself to start packing.

The kids in the village had already begun school, and Peter was feeling their absence. I felt it as well. I was used to the sound of their voices at play; their calls and laughter had disappeared. What I heard instead surprised me. I heard cranes.

Once, when I was a teenager, my father and I were walking to a section of the Madison River in Yellowstone Park when we came upon a pair of nesting sandhill cranes. We frightened them and they took flight. In unison they immediately started to make their unique and ancient cry. It is an unforgettable call. Cranes don't quack or twitter. They produce a great musical stuttering noise from the back of their throats. One of the pair landed about a hundred yards to our right and acted as if hurt, in an effort to lure us away from the nest, which must have been within feet of where we were standing. Had we been predators we might have gone after the "wounded" crane, hoping to get a bigger easier meal. I admired this valiant effort to protect the nest and watched in amazement as the bird limped and tripped, one wing tucked in and the other fanned out. My father and I made for the river so that we would not continue to disturb the crane parents. Within minutes the cranes quieted and returned to the nest, hidden from view.

Hearing that same call years later and thousands of miles away awoke fond memories, not only of the birds but of that day of fishing the Madison with my father. I can't recall what we caught—or even whether we caught anything at all. What I remember is sunshine, walking in a marsh, and the tall figure of my father ahead of me, leading me to the river. I always felt safe when my father was with me, and we always had a good day together when we went fishing

The Gimdalen cranes were Eurasian cranes that had been nesting and raising their young near the village for most of the summer. Now they were getting ready to return to Africa for the winter and were busily filling up on potatoes from the surrounding fields before departure. The cranes had been so quiet all summer that I hadn't even known they were there, not until they had begun relating their restlessness to be on their way south. I was in the house the first time I heard their unmistakable call. I dashed to the front porch just in time to see two adults and their two adolescent offspring lift from the potato field several lots away and fly over our house. Their six-foot wings pumped the air; their long bodies and fully extended legs made them look like bodysurfers in the sky.

I have always liked knowing that cranes mated for life. They are thought to bring good luck. In Japan, they are symbols of long life and a happy marriage. In Vietnam, cranes are believed to carry the souls of the dead to heaven. Cranes have inhabited the earth for over thirty million years. Perhaps there *is* something magical about them. At least they know how to survive.

We heard the cranes the rest of the week, making their melancholy cries from the fields. Then, just a few days before I was to leave, we stopped hearing them. The whine of chain saws and the deep roar of a tractor in the potato fields had replaced their cries. The bang of rifles at a range a mile away echoed off the hillsides throughout the late afternoon. These were the sounds of a village changing seasons.

Before returning to the States, Lars would winterize the house. He would tape the cracks in the windows to keep out drafts of freezing air, and he would close off the second story, so that the heat we had to leave on would not be "a fire for the crows." Finally, he would shut off the water. Carl-Åke would have a key, and would check on our house during the winter.

Our house. We owned a house in Sweden. The idea was still so new. We had a place to return to. That meant we would return.

The day before Peter and I left Gimdalen, I went to the river, stood on the bridge, and watched the waters of Idsjö-strömmen wash away from me. The sky was overcast. I could see a few grayling below, their tails swaying gently back and forth to hold themselves in the current. It looked as if they were waving good-bye. No one was in the first windbreak. The fire ring was cold. Fly rods, usually stored on the wind-break roof—the reels jutting off the eave—were gone. I thought about the fishermen who had made coffee over the open fire, and could almost see them, sitting and standing, waders rolled to their waists, speaking softly (or not at all), watching for the coffee to boil and for the fish to rise.

I thought about the smell of firs after they had been warmed by the sun; the taste of the blueberries that had been picked and eaten along the trail to the second windbreak; the grayling's metallic-blue-green body and magenta dorsal fin. I wanted to inhale the forest and the memories of birch-wood smoke, the sight of swifts beneath blue skies, the grayling at the end of my line, and hold my breath for one of those long winter days when I could exhale and have the summer reappear and renew me. Months would pass before I would touch and taste and smell a Swedish summer again.

I turned toward the house.

———

WHEN THE IMMIGRATION OFFICER handed me back my passport and said, "Welcome home," I was surprised by how I felt. I thanked him and took my passport as if receiving an award. I looked at its navy-blue cover with the gold lettering, the drawing of the eagle with the olive branch in one talon and a bundle of arrows in the other. I had never felt American before. How could I be classified as a citizen of only one country when I had already started to miss the smell of a birch-wood fire, the colors of Idsjöströmmen on a sunny day, and the fly fishers from Stockholm with their crumpled hats? On the other hand, I *was* curious to know whether the hopper fishing had been any good that year on the Madison; if the cutthroats in the park were still biting; and if streamer fishing for brown trout had started on the Yellowstone. I'd know soon.

Postscript

"WHAT IS HE SAYING?" I asked.

Lars shushed me with a wave of his hand. We were back in Bozeman and Lars was on the phone with Torbjörn, the carpenter who was going to renovate the kitchen and first floor of our house in Gimdalen. He would be working all winter, stripping the house to its bare walls, insulating them, punching out a place for a new window by the stairs, plumbing and installing a bathroom, laying linoleum, painting, wallpapering, installing appliances. I had not met Torbjörn.

"Tell him to send color samples."

My request was met by another dismissive wave of the hand.

I could tell the conversation was winding down. I wanted to interrupt again, to ask questions, but knew I would only get waved at.

"So what did he say?" I asked when Lars hung up.

"Everything will be finished by the time we arrive in May."

"What kind of cabinets are we getting for the kitchen?"

"We have decided that the cabinets will be white with blue trim. They are very nice."

"Who's 'we'?"

"Don't you remember? I showed you the pictures and you liked the cabinets very much."

"Yes, but I didn't know that it was decided. I think we should see more."

"What's wrong with what we looked at?"

"Nothing, it's just that I'm used to looking at more choices."

"We have measured and there are only certain places the sink, stove, countertops, and refrigerator can go. The cabinet model we have chosen will work there."

"I think we need to talk about this."

The rest of the morning was spent with graph paper, a notebook, and Lars trying to comfort me by saying things like, "That is standard, everyone knows how many outlets need to be in a room."

We finally agreed about the kitchen design, where the bathroom would go, how the office and dining room would be organized. But for me there were still unanswered questions and Torbjörn didn't speak English.

"Why do all the walls have to be papered? Why can't we

paint them? How can we really tell if the colors go together?"

Lars held steady. "That is standard, everyone knows you must have wallpaper on the walls, that the ceiling should be white."

"But Lars, somewhere in Sweden they must have a place where people go to pick out wallpaper and paint. And in that place are books put out by the wallpaper manufacturers, and displays put out by the paint companies so people will know what to buy. Don't they have places like that in Sweden?"

"Yes, at the hardware store."

"Yes, but—*I want samples!*"

Two weeks later Torbjörn sent samples in a business-size envelope: wallpaper print in Carl Larsson Red or Carl Larsson Blue for the kitchen; a similar print in the same color choices for the dining room. Over the fax came copies of the specs for the stove, refrigerator, washing machine, and dryer that Torbjörn had picked out for us.

"I like blue for the kitchen and dining room."

And with that I dropped the faxes and the envelope with the samples on Lars's desk. If I had learned anything from living in Sweden, it was about the sanity of simplicity. If I didn't like how the remodel turned out, at least Lars and Torbjörn would. If worse came to worst, they could move in together. Neither of them would complain about the decor.

"If something gets messed up, he'll just have to fix it," I declared.

Torbjörn finished on time and when we arrived the following May we walked into a structure that could flush, wash, and heat. The only thing I had to have repainted was the entryway. It was pink—pink like a stomach remedy (I hadn't seen a sample). The kitchen was perfect. The dining room was perfect. The office was perfect. The bathroom (I wanted to make it into a shrine) was perfect; it had a toilet, a sink, a shower, and a washer and dryer—all in the space of a walk-in closet. We slept on mattresses in the office again that summer, but made plans to finish the second floor, where we would create a master bedroom, a bedroom for Peter, a family room, and an office for me under the eaves.

Before I left for the States I made a trip to the hardware store and found the sample books, all three of them. I made my choice for wallpaper and found matching paints. Everything about the second phase of the remodel proceeded smoothly. And something else went smoothly as well—that winter in Bozeman, in front of a roaring fire in the fireplace lounge at the Gallatin Gateway Inn, Lars and I were married.

Acknowledgments

Heartfelt thanks to my agent, Carole Bidnick: You were prayers answered.

To my editor, Tim Bent: Thank you for believing in this story, for encouraging it to be told, and for watching over it.

Thank you to special friend Gwen Petersen, for reading, critiquing, and keeping me honest. To Mikael Larsson, for conversation, inspiration, encouragement, and the wonderful illustrations for this book. To Arthur Coffin and Sheila Vosen-Shorten, for looking me in the eye and asking for more. To Linda Schlossberg—a woman with a magic pen. To Peter, for following me on this great adventure. To Lilly Persson, *min speciella svenska lärare.* To my Swedish family, for opening their hearts and inviting me in: Magnus, Fredrik, Christina, Lennart,

Sara, Dennis, and Jonas, and especially Eva. To Idsjöströmmen, for calling me over the ocean. To the people of Gimdalen: Thank you for making me feel at home. And to Lars-Åke, forever and always.